SPECIAL SERIES

BASIC

Skill Builders Handbook

RAY BECK DENISE CONRAD PEGGY ANDERSON

Copyright © 1995 by Ray Beck,
Denise Conrad, and Peggy Anderson
All rights reserved.

05 04 03 02 01   09 08 07 06 05

No portion of this book, in whole or in part, may be reproduced
by any means without the express written permission of the publisher.

ISBN #1-57035-048-5

Edited by Maureen Adams
Text layout and cover design by Susan Krische

Printed in the United States of America

Published and Distributed by

SOPRIS
WEST

4093 Specialty Place • Longmont, Colorado 80504 • (303) 651-2829
http://www.sopriswest.com

16HANDBK/10-01/KEN/1M

PREFACE

About This Handbook

In search of new and better ways to teach students who are having difficulty, many of us from time to time have been caught up in what seems to be "in vogue." During the fifties there was drill. In the 1960s and 1970s we built schools without walls in hopes of self-discovery. Then there was modern math. In the 1980s and 1990s we moved to computerized instruction and site-based management. More recently Whole Language seems to have taken the field by storm, and it goes on and on. However, through all these educational fads, two principles of classroom learning have survived.

One: The authors have observed that accomplished students are ones who have practiced the skill **to a level of automaticy**. When students are in command of the skill, they **maintain** the skill, **transfer** the skill, and can **generalize** the skill. Follow the students who are accomplished athletes, musicians, actors, writers, readers, spellers, mathematicians, etc., and you will find students who have practiced the skill over and over and over.

Two: The authors have also observed that accomplished teachers are the ones who, among a host of attributes, have **closely monitored** the performance of their students. Follow teachers of skilled students, and you will find teachers that have monitored performance directly and continually. Most importantly, they have made instructional decisions from the students' performance data.

The intent of this handbook is to capture the skill, knowledge, and experience of three educators who, for over 20 years, have followed skilled teachers in both special and regular education environments. As teachers, school psychologists, and administrators, the authors share their experiences from a national Precision Teaching project, as well as the more recent, state-of-the-art principles of skill building.

This handbook provides the user with a step-by-step guide to implementing many of the basic principles of Precision Teaching. The focus, however, is on helping teachers, students, and parents use the series of Skill Builder Sheets designed to help students practice a skill to the point of proficiency. In addition, the manual helps teachers monitor and make instructional and curricular decisions based on student performance data.

—The Authors

CONTENTS

CHAPTER 1
Introduction and Overview 1
What Is It? 1
For Whom Is It Intended? 2
What Is Its Origin? 2
Does It Work? 3
What Is in It for Students? 3
What Is in It for Teachers? 4
What Are the Key Elements? 4
The Steps of *Basic Skill Builders* 14

CHAPTER 2
Selecting a Skill 21
Common Ties Between the *Basic Skill Builders* Model and the
    Effective Schools Research 23
Selecting the Skill 23
Getting Started 24
Other Considerations 25
Slice Back 26
Other Factors to Consider When Selecting the Skill 28
Implementing Learning Channels 29
Skill Builder Sheets 31
Curriculum Areas 32
Curriculum Areas for Which Skill Builder Sheets Are Not Available . . . 32
Setting Aims and Using Proficiency Standards 33
Establishing Expectations 34

CHAPTER 3
Practicing the Skill 37
- Common Ties Between the *Basic Skill Builders* Model and the
  Effective Schools Research 39
- The Relationship Between Tool Skills and Basic Skills 39
- Learning Channels and Their Effect on Practice 40
- Opportunities for Practice 41
- Using Skill Builders Sheets for Different Curricular Areas 41

CHAPTER 4
Monitoring the Skill 55
- Monitoring Performance 57
- Common Ties Between the *Basic Skill Builders* Model and the
  Effective Schools Research 57
- Effective Monitoring 58
- Tracking Student Performance 58

CHAPTER 5
Deciding on the New Skill 69
- Introduction 71
- Common Ties Between the *Basic Skill Builders* Model and the
  Effective Schools Research 71
- Indications of a Needed Change 72
- Deciding What Kind of Changes Should Be Made 74
- Stalled Learning 77
- Final Thought 78

CHAPTER 6
Managing the Skill 79
- Steps Before Classroom Implementation 81
- Organizational Suggestions for Getting Started 83
- In Summary 87

Introduction and Overview

> - What is it?
> - For whom is it intended?
> - What is its origin?
> - Does it work?
> - What is in it for students?
> - What is in it for teachers and parents?
> - What are the elements?

WHAT IS IT?

Basic Skill Builders is a collection of one-minute Skill Builder Sheets, a set of classroom procedures that utilize one-minute timed practices, and measurement guidelines that allow for data-based instructional and curricular decision making. Together these tools and concepts result in helping students become proficient in the basic skills of math, reading, and language arts. The concepts presented are well represented in the professional literature and are repeatedly promoted in the *Effective Schools Research*. Also presented are principles of learning found in model classrooms and best practices. The following are some classroom practices commonly found in the *Effective Schools Research* and *Basic Skill Builders*:

- Clear and high expectations
- Sequential curriculum
- Student tasks match teacher objectives
- Opportunities to respond
- Immediate feedback
- Monitor performance
- Data-based decisions
- Incentives and rewards

This skill building model can be used in conjunction with other instructional approaches, as long as these approaches have some evidence of effectiveness. The tenets of *Basic Skill Builders* are proven principles of measurement, repeated practice, memorization, and automaticity.

CHAPTER 1

FOR WHOM IS IT INTENDED?

Basic Skill Builders is for students who have trouble:

- Learning the skill
- Maintaining the skill
- Generalizing the skill

This skill building model is for teachers and parents who believe that students can learn better when high expectations are set, curriculum is presented in a visually consistent format, and students are provided with numerous opportunities to practice. For students with basic skill problems, this model offers them clear expectations, no surprises with curriculum presentation, and plenty of opportunities to reach objectives.

Basic Skill Builders is also for teachers or parents who believe that in order to be successful in academic settings or the world of work, one has to be "fluent" in basic skills. Further, students must not only be accurate, but also be able to quickly complete a task. Ultimately, a student who is engaged in higher-level thinking, abstract reasoning, and creativity will have a command of basic skills in math, reading, spelling, and other language arts.

Finally, *Basic Skill Builders* is for teachers or parents who find that some students, particularly those with learning difficulties, do not always respond favorably to current Whole Language approaches.

WHAT IS ITS ORIGIN?

Basic Skill Builders shares a rich history with the field of applied behavioral analysis and Precision Teaching. Ogden R. Lindsley, Professor Emeritus, University of Kansas, and the inventor of Precision Teaching, is credited with significantly influencing the thinking behind *Basic Skill Builders*. In addition, Harold Kuzelmann and Eric Haughton, students of Lindsley's, had a profound effect on *Basic Skill Builders* and helped shape the concepts of one-minute timed practices, the Learning Channel matrix, fluency, and tool skills.

Perhaps the greatest influence on the concepts presented in this handbook results from the development and subsequent dissemination of the Great Falls, Montana Public Schools' **Sacajawea Plan** in the 1970s and 1980s. It was during this period that a great many teacher-generated skill sheets were developed, tested, and used with both special and regular education students. The resulting materials in the Skill Builders Sheets were tried and judged by teachers to be a significant determinant in remediating basic skill deficits in students with learning disabilities. The same concepts and materials were used in regular classrooms across all grade levels to help students become fluent and bring their skills to a level of automaticity. The principles promoted in this handbook and its accompanying materials have a strong theoretical base as well as practical application in both the classroom and home.

DOES IT WORK?

Yes, it works. Longitudinal studies conducted in public school settings led the U.S. Department of Education to validate the model as a proven practice in both special and regular education. Students under the Sacajawea Plan outdistanced their counterparts between 20 and 40 percentile points in reading, math, and spelling. In addition to showing significant growth in the basic skills of reading, math, and spelling, students using the *Basic Skill Builders* model demonstrated:

- Better retention across time
- Better transfer of skills to more difficult tasks
- Better generalization

The Sacajawea Plan remained one of the longest federally sponsored programs in recent history. For over 12 years the Department of Education supported the project as it disseminated the concept to over 8,000 educators in 44 states and three Canadian provinces. Over 153,000 students were impacted. Further evidence of effectiveness has been reported in the *Journal of Precision Teaching*, a periodical dedicated to research in setting high expectations, conducting one-minute timed practices, monitoring learning, and building fluency.

WHAT IS IN IT FOR STUDENTS?

First of all, it is fun! Students not only enjoy the challenge of one-minute timings, but take pride in monitoring their daily progress toward clear and high expectations. Students know and benefit from good instructional environments. The skill building model includes:

- High expectations
- Clear objectives
- Sequenced curriculum with consistent format
- Numerous opportunities to practice
- One-minute timed practices
- Immediate feedback
- Visual display of progress
- Shared decision making
- Incentives and rewards

The following notes in Figure 1-1 are what students in Great Falls, Montana say about *Basic Skill Builders*:

Figure 1-1
Students' Comments

WHAT IS IN IT FOR TEACHERS?

Teachers like and use *Basic Skill Builders* because the students like it, and there is an immediate and positive change in student performance. It is manageable because:

- The students can do most of the procedures on their own, such as:
    - Take their own timings
    - Score and record their performance
    - Assist in data decisions
- There is a preestablished set of objectives and expectations (aims).
- There is a set of established curricula in the form of Skill Builder Sheets.
- There is direct and continuous monitoring of each student's learning
- There is a set of decisions rules that accompany the monitoring.
- The entire procedure requires no more than 15 minutes per day.

WHAT ARE THE KEY ELEMENTS?

There are ten elements that comprise the *Basic Skill Builders* model. The principles that guide the implementation have not only been well documented through research, but more importantly, have been found to be practical and effective in the classroom.

A brief rationale and explanation is offered to familiarize the first-time user with the terminology. One way of acquainting teachers and parents is to illustrate relationships and explain the tenets of *Basic Skill Builders*. It should be mentioned, however, that these will be reviewed in more detail in subsequent chapters. The key elements are:

- **Mastery and Proficiency** (fluency)—What is the relationship between mastery and proficiency?

  Proponents of mastery learning often focus on accuracy without much attention to fluency or speed. In *Basic Skill Builders* the authors promote proficiency that embraces both accuracy and speed. In this model students need to be more than 80% accurate to demonstrate a level of fluency. Once they reach a state of accuracy plus speed (i.e., proficiency), students find they are more comfortable with the skill, they are able to maintain the skill, transfer the skill to more difficult tasks, and can generalize the skill to other tasks.

  When students move beyond mastery to proficiency (fluency), they are found to be more attentive, stay with a task longer, and are resistant to distractions. In other words, they are in command.

- **Basic Skills and Tool Skills**—What is the difference between basic skills and tool skills?

  In the simplest form, basic skills are those skills necessary to survive in traditional academic settings. They are often referred to as the three "R"s (reading, writing, and arithmetic). We consider basic skills to be those fundamental skills necessary to demonstrate grade-level competency in areas such as reading, math, handwriting, spelling, grammar, geography, map skills, etc.

  Tool skills are those skills that are prerequisite to the basic skills. They allow students the freedom to improve the basic skill. For example, a tool skill of "say sounds" might be the prerequisite to the basic skill of "say words" in a fifth grade reading passage. "Write letters" may be the tool skill to "write dictated words" in spelling. Prior to students quickly responding to written math problems, they must have fluency in "writing numbers."

  Studies have long suggested that a strong relationship exists between students' tool skills and basic skills. We find that students showing proficiency in tool skills are more likely to demonstrate good basic skills. Figure 1-2 is an example of two students performing two separate tool skills. In the example, first graders are asked to look at a series of numbers and then reproduce the numbers as quickly as possible. Both are told they will have one minute to do as many as they can. The first student (Polly) demonstrates an appropriate age- and grade-level tool skill in writing numbers and letters. The second student (Matthew) shows tool skill deficits in writing numbers and hearing letters. Math facts and spelling words are in the future, however, in the case of Matthew it is clear that he does not have the tool skill necessary to successfully complete the basic skills of math and spelling. These tool skills will eventually have a direct bearing on the basic skills of math and spelling.

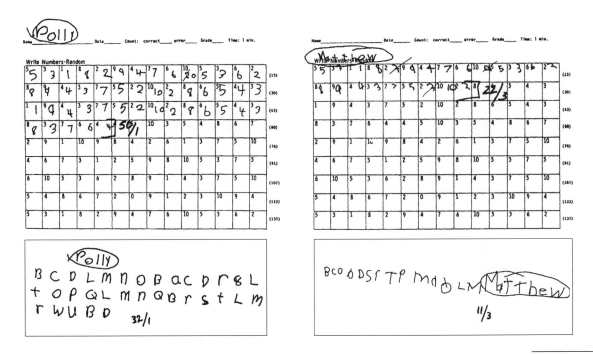

Figure 1-2
Examples of Polly's and Matthew's Tool Skills

- **Learning Channels**—What are Learning Channels?

Learning Channels are an arrangement of sensory modalities and statements that, when applied to instruction, are much easier to understand than the more traditional processing constructs. Simply stated, Learning Channels are a statement of how students receive and express information. There is an Input side and an Output side. Figure 1-3 is a matrix illustrating the idea of Learning Channels:

Input	Output
See	Say
Hear	Write
Think	Mark
Touch	Do

Figure 1-3
Learning Channels

On the Input side, it is believed that most academic demands require students to take information and material in through either the visual or auditory channel. For example, they are often required to look at or "see" a problem before responding. Also, there are occasions where they "hear" words, problems, or directions before responding. In some instances they are given tasks that do not require the eyes or the ears, but rather are asked to "think" before demonstrating the skill. An example of the latter might include, "Think of a reason for start of the Civil War."

Output requires that students somehow demonstrate or express the skill by either "saying" an answer, "writing" an answer, "marking" an answer, or following a direction ("doing"). Examples might include writing the answers to math facts, saying words aloud in a short reading passage, writing the dictated spelling words, or marking the pronouns in sentences.

Combining the Input with the Output, or expressive channel, gives us combinations such as those presented in Figure 1-4:

Input	Output
See	Say oral reading passages
See	Write answers to mixed math facts
See	Mark pronouns
Hear	Say answers to mixed math facts
Hear	Write answers to mixed math facts
Hear	Write dictated words
Think	Say add facts: combinations equal to 18
Think	Write add facts: combinations equal to 18

Figure 1-4
Input/Output

The greatest use of the Learning Channel matrix (Figure 1-4) is the visual display of the combinations possible when working with students experiencing specific modality problems. For example, if a student is an auditory learner, Skill Builder Sheets and instruction can be directed toward the Hear to Write or Hear to Say channels. Skill Builder Sheets can also be used to practice and measure different modalities. For example, a math fact sheet (see Figure 1-5) designed to have students practice sums to ten in addition could be used as a: See to Write, See to Say, Hear to Write, or a Hear to Say (see Figure 1-6). It is like exercising muscles: the more channels that are exercised, the stronger the skill becomes.

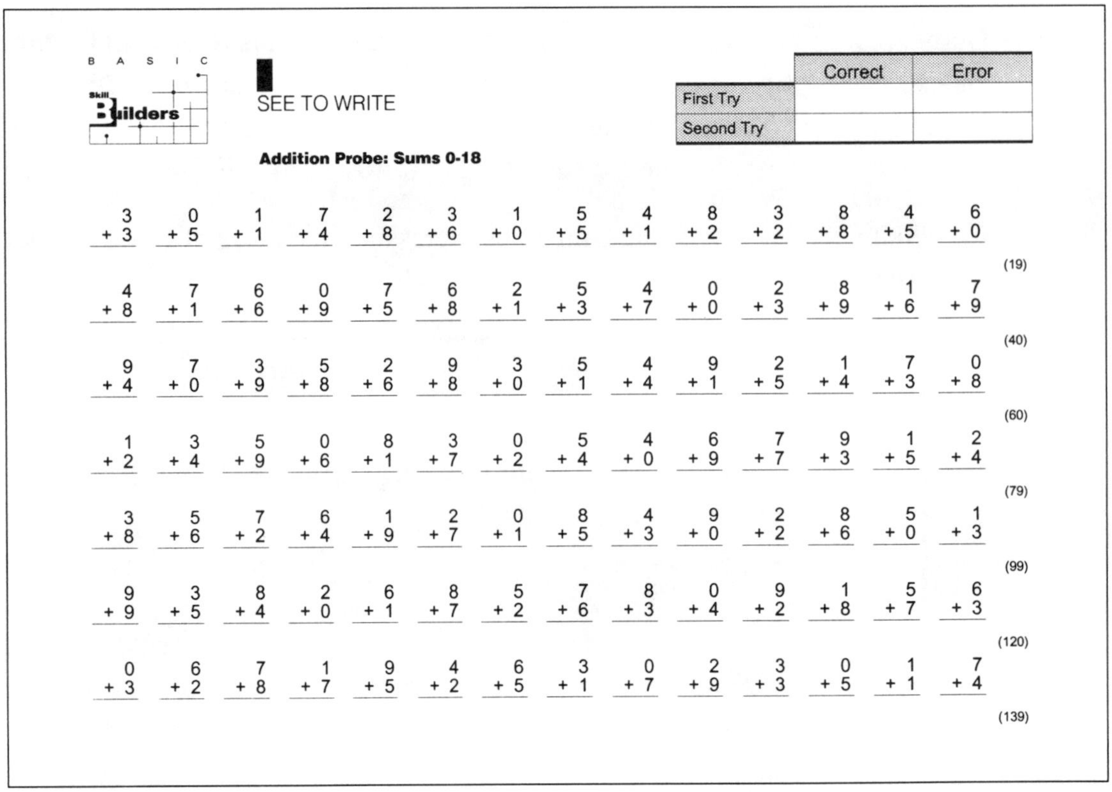

BASIC Skill Builders

SEE TO WRITE

	Correct	Error
First Try		
Second Try		

Addition Probe: Sums 0-18

3 + 3	0 + 5	1 + 1	7 + 4	2 + 8	3 + 6	1 + 0	5 + 5	4 + 1	8 + 2	3 + 2	8 + 8	4 + 5	6 + 0	(19)
4 + 8	7 + 1	6 + 6	0 + 9	7 + 5	6 + 8	2 + 1	5 + 3	4 + 7	0 + 0	2 + 3	8 + 9	1 + 6	7 + 9	(40)
9 + 4	7 + 0	3 + 9	5 + 8	2 + 6	9 + 8	3 + 0	5 + 1	4 + 4	9 + 1	2 + 5	1 + 4	7 + 3	0 + 8	(60)
1 + 2	3 + 4	5 + 9	0 + 6	8 + 1	3 + 7	0 + 2	5 + 4	4 + 0	6 + 9	7 + 7	9 + 3	1 + 5	2 + 4	(79)
3 + 8	5 + 6	7 + 2	6 + 4	1 + 9	2 + 7	0 + 1	8 + 5	4 + 3	9 + 0	2 + 2	8 + 6	5 + 0	1 + 3	(99)
9 + 9	3 + 5	8 + 4	2 + 0	6 + 1	8 + 7	5 + 2	7 + 6	8 + 3	0 + 4	9 + 2	1 + 8	5 + 7	6 + 3	(120)
0 + 3	6 + 2	7 + 8	1 + 7	9 + 5	4 + 2	6 + 5	3 + 1	0 + 7	2 + 9	3 + 3	0 + 5	1 + 1	7 + 4	(139)

Figure 1-5
Sample Skill Builder Sheet

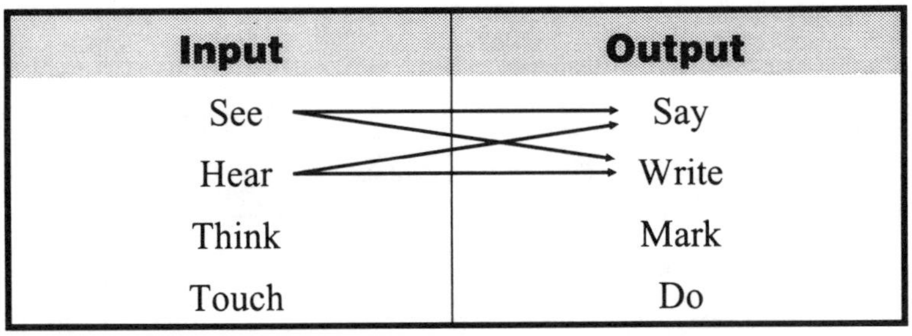

Figure 1-6
Learning Channels

- **Proficiency Standards and Aims**—How are proficiency standards different from aims?

  Proficiency standards are levels that when reached suggest a high probability that students will remember the skill over time. Furthermore, they will be able to apply the skill to a more difficult task, and be able to generalize the skill to other areas outside or removed from the current demands. Aims are used to give students goals or objectives to work toward. Aims are often considered intermediate goals to achieve while working toward the proficiency standard.

  Proficiency standards have been typically established through research and have been documented, when reached, to preserve the skill across time and environments. Proficiency standards might seem high initially, however, research and classroom experience have clearly demonstrated that the higher the expectation, the higher the probability students will perform better than if there were little or no expectation.

Proficiency standards help guide students to an expectation level where the skill becomes automatic, thus instantly available. In most instances the skill has to be practiced and demonstrated at a level or frequency that is higher than what would be expected in the environment outside the classroom. Both proficiency standards and aims can be established by either using existing lists (see Chapter 2), or through examining the fluency levels of others considered to be proficient. See Figure 1-7 for examples of proficiency standards and aims.

> *"If you are to hit your mark, you must aim above the target."*
> —Longfellow

Proficiency standards might look like the following:

Task	Proficiency Standard
See to Say words in context	200 words per minute
See to Write add facts to 18	80 digits per minute
Hear to Write dictated words	20 words per minute

Aims are temporary goals and might look like the following:

Task	Aims
See to Say words in context	100 words per minute
See to Write add facts to 18	50 digits per minute
Hear to Write dictated words	10 words per minute

Figure 1-7
Proficiency Standards and Aims

- **Skill Builder Sheets**—Why are Skill Builder Sheets more user friendly than traditional skill exercises?

Several of the best features of the Skill Builder Sheets are that the format is consistent, the sequence follows a logical progression, and they were developed by teachers. One of the most confusing demands put on students, particularly students with learning difficulties, is to present curriculum with multi-dimensional demands. Math worksheets are some of the best examples. Figure 1-8 is an example taken from a current fifth grade math workbook.

CHAPTER 1

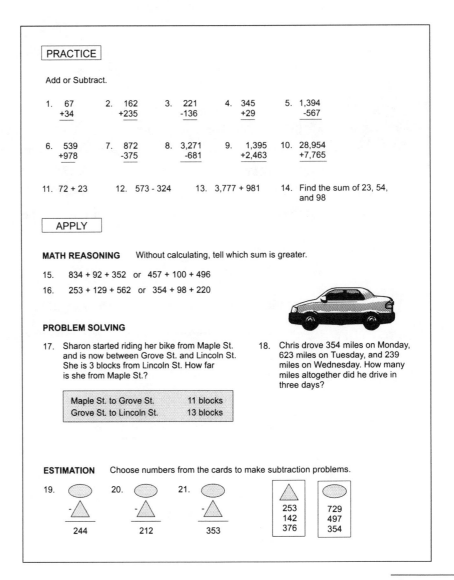

Figure 1-8
Example of math worksheet

Note how the demands change from one part of the activity to another. To students with visual organization problems, this type of curriculum is devastating. As an alternative, examine the Skill Builder Sheet presented in Figure 1-9. In this case, and on most of the other Skill Builder Sheets, the format is consistent. There are no attempts to fool students with pages of cleverly designed multi-dimensional constructs. The *Basic Skill Builders*' motto is: **keep it visually consistent** and **present it in sequence**.

BASIC Skill Builders

SEE TO WRITE

	Correct	Error
First Try		
Second Try		

Multiplication: Multiply by 3 (Answers 15-27)

3 x 7	9 x 3	8 x 3	6 x 3	7 x 3	3 x 9	5 x 3	7 x 3	7 x 3	3 x 9	3 x 7	6 x 3	7 x 3	3 x 8	9 x 3	(30)
3 x 7	8 x 3	3 x 6	7 x 3	3 x 9	3 x 8	3 x 9	3 x 6	3 x 7	8 x 3	3 x 6	7 x 3	3 x 8	9 x 3	6 x 3	(60)
3 x 8	7 x 3	3 x 9	8 x 3	6 x 3	3 x 6	8 x 3	3 x 7	9 x 3	3 x 8	6 x 3	3 x 9	5 x 3	3 x 6	6 x 3	(90)
3 x 8	7 x 3	3 x 9	8 x 3	6 x 3	3 x 6	8 x 3	3 x 7	9 x 3	3 x 8	6 x 3	3 x 9	5 x 3	3 x 6	6 x 3	(120)
3 x 9	7 x 3	3 x 8	6 x 3	3 x 6	7 x 3	3 x 7	8 x 3	3 x 9	9 x 3	3 x 8	9 x 3	3 x 9	8 x 3	3 x 7	(150)
9 x 3	3 x 6	7 x 3	3 x 8	6 x 3	3 x 7	6 x 3	5 x 3	9 x 3	3 x 8	7 x 3	3 x 4	8 x 3	3 x 7	9 x 3	(180)

Figure 1-9
Skill Builder Sheet

Another difference between the *Basic Skill Builders* approach and the more traditional one, is the logical order in which the Skill Builder Sheets are presented. A good deal of energy was spent assuring that the curriculum was sequenced to ensure that even students with severe disabilities could find success. One of the most striking results of curriculum slices, settings aims, and one-minute timed practices is that students stay focused (on task) and are not easily distracted.

- **Rate Measurement vs. Percentage**—Why is rate measurement more appropriate than percentage?

The difficulty with percentage as a classroom metric is that it gives no indication of the time required for students to complete the task. On the other hand, rate uses time as a constant denominator and expresses corrects and errors as number per minute. In formulaic terms, rate = frequency of response, divided by time. In the Skill Builder Sheets, student responses are expressed as number of corrects and errors per minute.

The bottom line is that rate is a much more sensitive measure because it takes frequency of response and time into account. When fluency (i.e., accuracy and speed) is a desired academic outcome, rate is more critical and sensitive than other classroom metrics.

- **One-Minute Timed Practices and Rate of Response**—What is the relationship between one-minute timed practices and rate of response?

One of the themes that surfaces in the *Effective Schools Research* is **time spent on task**. This concept, more than any other, is closely associated with student performance and academic growth. The use of the Skill Builder Sheets, paired with one-minute timed practices give students repeated opportunities (practice) to respond, almost to a point of over-learning a skill.

One-minute timed practices have the further advantage of keeping students highly motivated. With a 60-second limit to the task, they are not faced with long, tedious, and arduous tasks. Students also know that multiple one-minute timed practices are available if they do not score well, or they simply wish to try to better their scores. In most situations students attempt at least two timed practices and take the best of scores for the daily mark.

Again, one-minute timed practices keep students on task and typically free from distractions. Because these timings and the Skill Builder Sheets are so manageable, parents can get involved at home.

- **Acquisition and Practice**—What effect does practice have on acquisition of a new skill?

Practice bridges the gap between learning a skill (acquisition) and fluently demonstrating the skill (proficiency). The acquisition of a skill is the first in a three-step series of development. In the initial stage the instructor teaches and demonstrates the skill. The second step involves the student and teacher practicing the skill together. The third and final stage involves the conditions of accuracy and speed, which is a statement of proficiency (fluency). An example would be, when given fifth grade mixed math facts, students demonstrated 90 correct responses per minute, with two errors. The students possess both accuracy and speed. Immediate feedback coupled with reward is integrated in the last two steps.

Perhaps a simpler way of viewing acquisition and its relationship with practice is through the idea of "I do it," "We do it," "You do it":

Acquisition Stage	
I do it	(Teacher demonstrates to the student)
We do it	(Teacher and student practice together)
Practice Stage	
You do it	(Student practices independently)

It is important to remember that practice has a significant effect on academic performance, but only **after** students have been taught and can demonstrate the skill. Remember that practice does not make perfect, perfect practice makes perfect.

- **Monitoring Performance and Decision Making**—How does monitoring performance and decision making fit into the *Basic Skill Builders* model?

  Monitoring student performance is another theme in the *Effective Schools Research*, however, tracking students is not enough. Performance data should never be gathered unless there is a plan to use the data for instructional or curricular decision making. It is not good enough to merely report scores, those data have to be used to decide whether changes in the instructional process or curriculum presentation are necessary.

  In the *Basic Skill Builders* model, performance data are taken directly from the curriculum, (as opposed to indirect measures from standardized testing), and are gathered daily. From the daily monitoring, patterns or pictures emerge and are visually displayed on charts. Once the patterns or pictures are analyzed, the teacher, or the teacher and student together, use a set of rules to determine if a change is needed. These rules comprise **If-Then** relationships. Consider the following matrix:

If	Then
If at aim for two days	Then change
If three days of little or no growth	Then change
If less than 25% growth each week	Then change

  The important point to keep in mind is that monitoring and tracking student performance is not sufficient. Data-based decisions must be made. Deciding what to do will be covered more extensively in Chapter 4 (Deciding on the New Skill).

- **The Standard Celeration Chart**—What is the difference between traditional graphs and the Standard Celeration Chart?

  The fundamental difference between a traditional graph and the Standard Celeration Chart used in *Basic Skill Builders*, is that the latter is standardized and shows proportional growth. Unlike equal interval graphs that can be expanded or reduced, the Standard Celeration Chart holds the vertical and horizontal scales constant. Another major difference between the two methods is that the Standard Celeration Chart is designed where the horizontal (rate) lines are logarithmic, while the vertical (day) lines are equal intervals—thus a semi-logarithmic chart.

  The advantage of a proportional chart and its display is that daily performance data can be analyzed and interpreted as percent of growth. A student who grows from 9 to 10 correct per minute demonstrates a 10% growth. Another student who grows from 90 to 100 also demonstrates an approximate 10% growth. When plotted on the Standard Celeration Chart, the degree or slope of the data is exactly the same for both students, suggesting they both grew proportionally the same (see Figure 1-10).

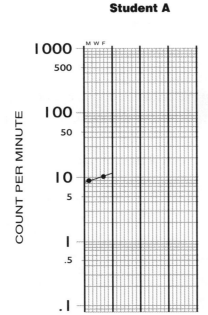

Figure 1-10
Standard Celeration Chart

The most important point, however, is that the Standard Celeration Chart can be used by students to visually display how their variations in daily performance can be translated in to a **picture of learning**. As a result, decisions and challenges for new tasks can be made based on these visuals.

THE STEPS OF *BASIC SKILL BUILDERS*

First, you must subscribe to the belief that teaching requires, among other things, setting clear expectations, providing opportunities to practice, and measuring learning. The latter is a big step considering the many day-to-day classroom demands and the volume of available curricular materials. Here are the five steps involved (including the chapters in this handbook that discuss the steps in depth) in the *Basic Skill Builders* model:

Step 1: **Selecting the Skill** (Chapter 2)

- Select a curriculum starting point
- Select the Learning Channel
- Select an aim

Step 2: **Practicing the Skill** (Chapter 3)

- Demonstrate by "I do it," "We do it," "You do it"
- Provide students with individual folders
- Provide daily opportunities to practice skill
- Provide feedback and rewards

Step 3: **Monitoring the Skill** (Chapter 4)

- Count and record corrects and errors
- Visually display performance and learning

Step 4: **Deciding on the New Skill** (Chapter 5)

- Analyze data and use rules
- Determine if the Skill Builder Sheet is:
    - Appropriate
    - Too hard
    - Too easy

Step 5: **Managing the Skill** (Chapter 6)

- Manage student plans by:
    - Providing a rationale
    - Providing materials
    - Establishing a routine
    - Promoting self-management

With a commitment and these five steps, teachers and parents will significantly help students **learn** the skill, **maintain** the skill, and **generalize** the skill.

The following chapters will explain in greater detail the five steps involved in *Basic Skill Builders*. In addition, this handbook will also examine the how-tos of implementation in order for this model to become second nature to you. As a bonus, you will have fun while being a witness to your students' learning.

The Five Steps of *Basic Skill Builders*

- Selecting the Skill ▼
- Practicing the Skill ▼
- Monitoring the Skill ▼
- Deciding on the New Skill ▼
- Managing the Skill ▼

Chapter 1

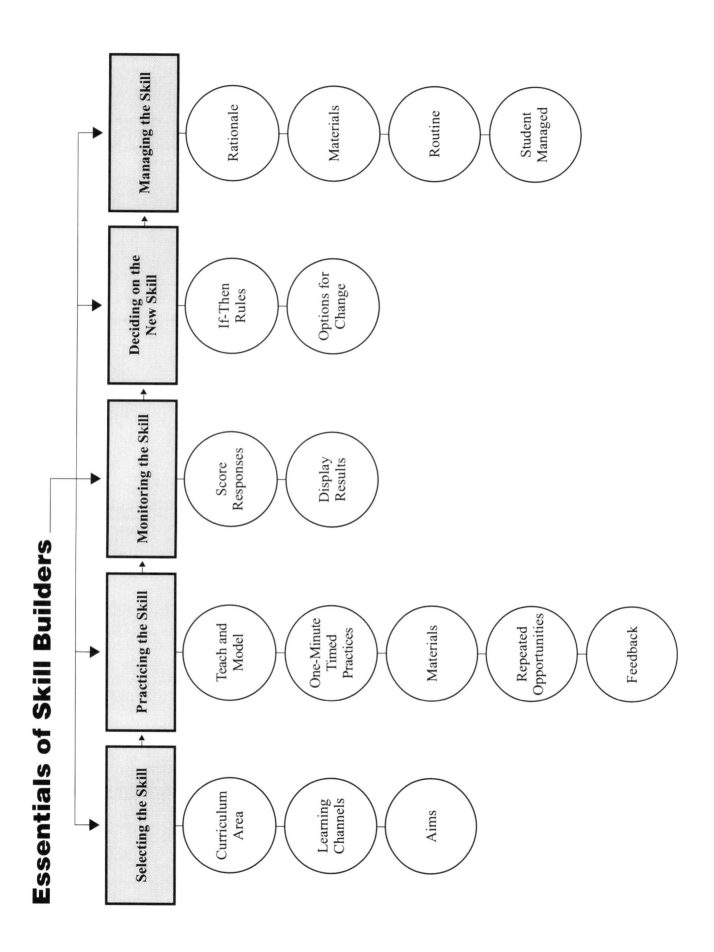

The Five Steps of *Basic Skill Builders*

- Selecting the Skill
- Practicing the Skill
- Monitoring the Skill
- Deciding on the New Skill
- Managing the Skill

CHAPTER 2

Considerations

- Curriculum Area
- Learning Channels
- Aims

Chapter 2

Selecting the Skill

- What are the steps involved in selecting skills and goals?
- What is a slice back?
- What types of skill sheets are available?

COMMON TIES BETWEEN THE *BASIC SKILL BUILDERS* MODEL AND THE *EFFECTIVE SCHOOLS RESEARCH*

Here is what the *Effective Schools Research* and *Basic Skill Builders* promote regarding the selection of a skill. The skill should:

- Have clear objectives
- Be matched to the objective
- Include high expectations
- Be presented with clear instructions
- Consider students' learning styles
- Consider tool (prerequisite) skills

SELECTING THE SKILL

When selecting the skill, you must choose:

- A general curriculum area
- A general skill area
- A specific skill

- A Learning Channel
- An aim

See Figure 2-1 for examples of what is involved when selecting the skill.

Select:				
General Curriculum	*General Skill*	*Specific Skill*	*Learning Channel*	*Aims/ Expectations*
Math	Math Computation	Add Facts (Sums 0-18)	See to Write Add Facts	80 Digits/min.
Reading	Oral Reading	Fifth Grade Reading Passage	See to Say Reading Passage	200 Words/min.
Spelling	Dictation	Fifth Grade Spelling Words	Hear to Write Spelling Words	15 Words/min.
Map Skills	Fifty United States	Abbreviations for Fifty States	Hear to Write State Abbreviations	50 State Abbreviations/min.
Language Arts	Grammar	Adjectives and Verbs	See to Mark Adjectives and Verbs	20 Adjectives and Verbs/min.

Figure 2-1
Skill Examples

GETTING STARTED

To begin the *Basic Skill Builders* process ask two questions: (1) **What is the skill** the students need to learn and (2) **how will it be demonstrated?** In the *Basic Skill Builders* model students perform skills accurately and fluently. In other words, students will have a command of skills that are immediately available across a variety of learning environments. If it is considered a lifelong skill (e.g., computation, writing, reading, etc.), the students need to be able to generalize it from academic settings to the real world.

In order to answer these two questions, first select the general curriculum area on which to focus. Skill Builder Sheets will aid in identifying skill deficit areas. Sheets are available in over ten curriculum areas, the most popular are:

- Math
- Reading
- Handwriting
- Map Skills
- Language Arts
- Science
- Social Studies

Once you have selected the curriculum focus, decide which **general skill** is required to enable students to work comfortably in a particular curriculum area(s). The skill might be reading aloud, completing simple addition and subtraction, or identifying the 50 states by writing the state abbreviations inside the borders of each state. Further steps include:

1. **Articulating the specific skill to a finer degree.** For example, you may request the skill of "add facts with sums 0-18." Math is the general curriculum, "add facts" is the general skill, and "sums 0-18" is the specific skill required to demonstrate competency.

2. **Deciding which Learning Channel students should use.** In Chapter 1, Learning Channels were described as a set of Input and Output modalities. The question when choosing a Learning Channel should be: Does the particular student learn better if the auditory channel is used, or does he/she seem to do better when using the visual channel? Perhaps the most important question should be: What channel is likely to be used in meeting classroom objectives?

3. **Setting aims (number of responses per minute) and expectations.** Aims should be set high enough so that the students are challenged, but low enough so that goals are within reach. Second, when students reach their aims, they should feel comfortable with the skill and should be able to perform it automatically. Aims can be set by using:

   - Existing proficiency standards
   - Intermediate goals
   - Other students of the same age level or grade level
   - Tool skills
   - Real-world expectations

OTHER CONSIDERATIONS

There are three other considerations to take into account when selecting the skill:

1. Be certain that the skill is **relevant**. Choose Skill Builder Sheets that are directly tied to the current curriculum. For instance, utilizing U.S. Map Skill Sheets may only be appropriate if you are currently working with curriculum content that focuses on geography or map skills pertaining to the United States.

2. Be certain that the skill is **essential**. Given the time constraints and many demands of the typical classroom, it is important to choose Skill Builder Sheets that provide practice and reinforcement on specific curricular objectives. In the case of students with disabilities, it may be important to chose Skill Builder Sheets that are directly tied to each student's IEP goals and objectives.

3. Be certain to select **large portions**. Measure and provide practice on the biggest portions of the curriculum as possible. Examples include:

- End-of-unit or entire chapter tests
- Skill clusters such as Add Facts 0-10, rather than Add 1s
- Reading a passage as opposed to isolated words
- The entire U.S. map, rather than just the New England states

The point is to chose a measurement condition (e.g., the entire U.S. map) as the unit of measurement, rather than each section of the country. You can still have students practice on individual states or groups of states, yet the daily measurement will be the number of states they can identify on the entire U.S. map.

SLICE BACK

If students are unable to show progress or even get started, the task might be too hard. You may have to consider a "slice back" to an easier activity. There are three levels to slice backs. The first level refers to a smaller segment or "slice" of the larger skill. For example:

If the original task is . . .	A slice back might be . . .
Mary writes answers to multiplication facts x 1 through x 5.	Mary writes answers to multiplication facts x 2.
Joe reads words in stories from a fifth grade reader.	Joe repeats the first five lines four times.
John writes state abbreviations on the US. map (see Figure 2-2).	John writes state abbreviations on map of the Central States (Figure 2-3).

Figure 2-2
U.S. Map

Figure 2-3
Central States Map

Another level of slice back has students step back to a task that is made much easier, and comes earlier in the skill sequence. For example:

If the original task is . . .	A slice back might be . . .
Alex reads time from clock faces to the five minute mark (e.g., 8:40, 11:35, etc.).	Alex reads time to the half hour.
Mary reads words in fourth grade stories.	Mary reads words in second grade stories.
Tommy writes state abbreviations on map of Western States (see Figure 2-4).	Tommy uses answer key to write abbreviations next to the name of each state (see Figure 2-5).

Figure 2-4
Western States Map

Basic Skill Builders

	Correct	Error
First Try		
Second Try		

SEE TO WRITE

Western States

Directions: Write Abbreviations.

Washington WA   Oregon OR   California CA   Nevada NV   Arizona AZ   New Mexico NM
Colorado CO   Utah UT   Idaho ID   Wyoming WY   Montana MT   Alaska AK   Hawaii HI

Washington	Oregon	California	Nevada	Arizona	(5)
New Mexico	Colorado	Utah	Idaho	Wyoming	(10)
Montana	Alaska	Hawaii	California	New Mexico	(15)
Arizona	Utah	Montana	Oregon	Wyoming	(20)
Colorado	Washington	Alaska	Nevada	Idaho	(25)
Utah	Hawaii	Oregon	Colorado	Nevada	(30)
California	Arizona	New Mexico	Washington	Montana	(35)
Idaho	Utah	Wyoming	Hawaii	Colorado	(40)
Washington	Alaska	Idaho	California	Alaska	(45)
Nevada	Wyoming	Oregon	Arizona	Utah	(50)

Figure 2-5
Western State Abbreviations

The third level of slice back requires looking at the skills that are prerequisite to the general (basic) skill. These are called **tool** skills. Example tool skills follow:

If the original task is . . .	A tool skill might be . . .
Mary writes multiplication answers x 5.	Mary repeatedly writes the numerals 1-10.
Jill prints the letters of her first and last name.	Jill repeatedly picks up a pencil, holds it in the writing position, makes a mark, and puts the pencil down.
Jack reads clock faces to the five minute mark.	Jack counts by 5s from 5 to 60.

OTHER FACTORS TO CONSIDER WHEN SELECTING THE SKILL

The task must be defined in clear and specific language. Rather than ask the student to go do his/her math, a better direction might be to "Write answers to facts: multiply by 1 through multiply by 5s." The second factor to keep in mind is that the task should be countable and repeatable. The following are examples of ambiguous, non-specific statements about students that are either difficult or impossible to quantify:

- "Mary is lazy."
- "Joe can't read."

- "Sue is a good math student."
- "John is learning disabled."

More appropriate and countable descriptions of student performance would include statements like:

- "Mary writes third grade spelling words at 5 per minute."
- "Joe reads fourth grade words at 70 per minute."
- "Sue write answers to add facts 0-18 at 75 per minute."
- "John writes state abbreviations on the U.S. map at 28 letters per minute."

In the above situations, one could both "describe" and "count" the behavior. The matrix below further illustrates this point:

If the task is . . .	The teacher could count . . .
Mary writes spelling words.	Words spelled or letters written.
Joe reads words from second grade basal.	Words read.
Sue writes answers to add facts 0-18.	Written answers or digits in answer (9 + 8 = 17); answer has two digits.
John writes state abbreviations on U.S. map.	Letter abbreviations written.

When counting it is important to count **both corrects** and **errors.** First of all, errors help teachers focus on specific instruction. Second, errors help both teachers and students select specific Skill Builder Sheets for practice exercises.

To review, the essential elements of selecting a skill include ensuring that:

- The skill is relevant and essential to skill objective.
- The skill represents a large portion of the curriculum.
- The skill is articulated in specific language.

IMPLEMENTING LEARNING CHANNELS

Earlier it was discussed how Learning Channels offer a clear and simple way of explaining which modality students use to receive details of the task demands, and then which modality is used to express their responses. For instance, the following represents possible Inputs:

Channel	Example
See	Seeing words on a page.
Hear	Hearing dictated words.
Think	Thinking of questions to ask about a story.

Basic Skill Builders

The following represents possible Outputs:

Channel	Example
Say	Saying words on a page.
Write	Writing dictated words.
Mark	Marking nouns and verbs.

Keep in mind that many of the Skill Builder Sheets are designed to exercise a combination of Learning Channels. For example, a student might be given a Skill Builder Sheet requiring students to add facts with sums 0-18 (see Figure 2-6).

BASIC Skill Builders

SEE TO WRITE

Addition Probe: Sums 0-18

	Correct	Error
First Try		
Second Try		

3 + 3	0 + 5	1 + 1	7 + 4	2 + 8	3 + 6	1 + 0	5 + 5	4 + 1	8 + 2	3 + 2	8 + 8	4 + 5	6 + 0	(19)
4 + 8	7 + 1	6 + 6	0 + 9	7 + 5	6 + 8	2 + 1	5 + 3	4 + 7	0 + 0	2 + 3	8 + 9	1 + 6	7 + 9	(40)
9 + 4	7 + 0	3 + 9	5 + 8	2 + 6	9 + 8	3 + 0	5 + 1	4 + 4	9 + 1	2 + 5	1 + 4	7 + 3	0 + 8	(60)
1 + 2	3 + 4	5 + 9	0 + 6	8 + 1	3 + 7	0 + 2	5 + 4	4 + 0	6 + 9	7 + 7	9 + 3	1 + 5	2 + 4	(79)
3 + 8	5 + 6	7 + 2	6 + 4	1 + 9	2 + 7	0 + 1	8 + 5	4 + 3	9 + 0	2 + 2	8 + 6	5 + 0	1 + 3	(99)
9 + 9	3 + 5	8 + 4	2 + 0	6 + 1	8 + 7	5 + 2	7 + 6	8 + 3	0 + 4	9 + 2	1 + 8	5 + 7	6 + 3	(120)
0 + 3	6 + 2	7 + 8	1 + 7	9 + 5	4 + 2	6 + 5	3 + 1	0 + 7	2 + 9	3 + 3	0 + 5	1 + 1	7 + 4	(139)

Figure 2-6
Add Facts 0-18

Using the Skill Builder Sheet in Figure 2-6 as an example, the sheet can be used as a:

- See to Write task—the students "see" (Input) a math fact and then "write" (Output) the answers.
- See to Say task—the students "see" (Input) a math fact and then "say" (Output) the answers.

Other examples of skills and the Learning Channels are:

- Hear to Write spelling words
- See to Say words (orally) in passage
- Think to Say ideas about democracy
- Think to Write facts about the solar system

Teachers should view the use of Learning Channels as an opportunity to introduce and reinforce skills by using different modalities. For example, if a student is having difficulty with a See to Write Channel, the teacher might change to a Hear to Write Channel.

Another example might be the student who is doing one-minute timed practices on Think to Write digits 0-9. The student who finds the task too hard might use a different channel and attempt a See to Trace or See to Copy numbers 0-9. The next step would be returning to the Think to Write digits 0-9.

SKILL BUILDER SHEETS

General curriculum areas have been divided into specific curriculum areas and include packets, with an average of 60 Skill Builder Sheets per packet. Examples include the following areas:

- Math:
    - Tool Skills—writing numbers
    - Basic Computation—addition, subtraction, multiplication, and division
    - Story Problems
    - Fractions
    - Decimals
    - Telling Time
    - Geometry—basic angles, figures
    - Measurements
    - Algebra

- Reading:
    - Tool Skills—letters, sounds
    - Vocabulary Words

- Handwriting:
    - Tool Skills—circles, slashes, pencil-holding
    - Manuscript—upper and lower case
    - Cursive—upper and lower case

- Language Arts:
    - Tool Skills
    - Grammar—parts of speech, punctuation
    - Concepts—basic

- Map Skills:
    - Tool Skills
    - U.S. Map—states, capitals

One of the major advantages of the *Basic Skill Builders* packets is that nearly all the Skill Builder Sheets are accompanied by answer sheets. Two benefits are obvious: first, students can self-correct thus relieving teachers of this task; second, immediate feedback is provided to students. Research has shown that the sooner students receive feedback, the more likely they are to demonstrate improvement.

CURRICULUM AREAS

When first getting started with *Basic Skill Builders*, consider the general curriculum area of math, for it is usually the easiest to implement. Also, it is helpful to administer a **probe**, which is a Skill Builder Sheet designed to test and/or investigate student performance on a combination of skills. A math probe might be presented that requires all four computational skills (addition, subtraction, multiplication, and division). You may want to examine the sheets after the students complete them and depending on the number of corrects and errors, decide the specific skill on which to concentrate. For example, if students were given a mixed math facts probe and skipped every division problem, you might want to select a further probe with only division problems. In this way you could determine whether students lack the skills, or merely skipped these particular problems because division took more time, or only missed problems where "9" was the divisor.

Administering a probe might also provide diagnostic evidence on whether students have the rate or fluency level commensurate with established aims. It might be that students should practice some tool skills (e.g., write numbers randomly) as well as work on the basic skill of mixed math facts.

CURRICULUM AREAS FOR WHICH SKILL BUILDER SHEETS ARE NOT AVAILABLE

In the area of reading it may be necessary to create Skill Builder Sheets that correspond to the basal or literature selections the students are studying. Skill Builder Sheet activities can be developed to accompany any reading series, children's book, or novel. When developing daily practice and skill building ideas, remember it is important to start with the biggest portion of the curriculum as possible.

The following are some suggestions for skill building activities in reading:

1. Students, if at all possible, should read directly from the book, as opposed to reading from a Skill Builder Sheet. This may involve students repeatedly reading the same passage, paragraph, sentence, or word list over several days. However, this repeated practice will have a positive effect.

2. When working with students using pre-primers or books with very few words on the page, you may have to put the sentences on Skill Builder Sheets, rather than reading directly from the book. This will eliminate the problem of turning pages.

   Be sure that the size and type of print is similar to that of the reading book. In addition, there should be at least 100 words on the page. If students finish before the one-minute timed practice is up, encourage them to begin again at the top of the page.

3. If students are having trouble reading words at 150-200 per minute, you may choose to change the format. For instance, students could repeatedly read the first paragraph, or the first 20-40 words. A pattern of higher frequencies and a more natural rhythm of conversational speech should become evident.

4. It may be necessary to slice back the curriculum and have students work with only new or unfamiliar vocabulary words. In this situation it is helpful to create short phrases where a new word is blended into the phrase. The phrases, however, are usually taken directly from a story and should include only three or four words. In addition, it is helpful to randomly place about ten phrases to a page (Skill Builder Sheet) and use several sheets, if necessary.

5. The smallest level of curriculum slices, other than slicing back to tool skills, is to develop Skill Builder Sheets with isolated words. To obtain this you create a sheet with no more than ten new words. Again the words are randomly placed on the page, appearing about the same number of times, with no more than 100 total on the sheet.

SETTING AIMS AND USING PROFICIENCY STANDARDS

Before students begin using one-minute Skill Builder Sheets, there should be clear expectations stating the level at which the task is considered **proficient**. This is a level where students will be able to fluently demonstrate the task. They will perform the skill accurately, smoothly, and with little or no hesitation. It is where **accuracy** plus **speed** are evident and the behavior becomes automatic.

When setting clear and high expectations, there are two terms that should be reviewed: aims and proficiency standards. As was discussed earlier, aims are presented to students as intermediate goals. In some instances, particularly for students who view long-range goals as unattainable, it might be more appropriate to set short-term aims. On the other hand, there are students who enjoy the challenge of very high expectations, and recognize that goals may be a long way off. Remember, aims are not carved in stone.

Proficiency standards are more closely aligned to set expectations. *Basic Skill Builders*' standards come from research conducted during the Sacajawea Plan, as well as other research projects across the country. These standards are levels of performance that when reached, seem to significantly increase the probability that students will be able to: (1) maintain the skill; (2) transfer the skill to more difficult tasks; and (3) generalize the skill across other environments.

ESTABLISHING EXPECTATIONS

To establish expectations you can either use existing proficiency standards or develop individual aims. It is probably less confusing if aims are used as the official terminology, and include proficiency standards under the aims "umbrella." This may sound a little disjointed, so the following will illustrate by using situations in math and reading. First, keep in mind that aims can be set by using:

- Existing Proficiency Standards
- Intermediate Goals
- Peer Performance
- Tool Skill Frequencies
- Real-World Expectations

The following proficiency aims for math are based on findings reported by the Sacajawea Plan.

Math Aims

Task Examples	Proficiency Standard Examples
See to Write Numbers (tracing)	20-40 digits/min.
See to Write Numbers	100-150 digits/min.
See to Write Math Facts	70-90 digits/min.

Intermediate goals can be set either by the teacher, or teachers, students, and parents in conferences. For example, it may be agreed that although the goal might be 70-90 digits per minute in double column addition, an intermediate aim will be 50 digits per minute.

Peer performance is often a fair and effective method for determining aims, particularly if there are no established proficiency standards, or little is known about the specific skill. For example, students might be working on a complicated math task where no proficiency standards exist. It is helpful to have three or four peers considered proficient take at least three timed practices. Average these students scores for the individual or class-wide aim.

Tool skill frequencies can often be a guide in setting aims for students. In math, students demonstrate tool skills through one-minute timed practices, or motor skills such as "write numbers randomly," or "write numbers sequentially." The highest score over three trials can be used as a guide to set an aim for math facts. You might consider backing off the tool skill score by approximately 20% for the math aim. These scores become more meaningful when you compare the tool skill frequency to the basic skill expectations. For example, it would seem unfair to set an aim of 70-90 digits per minute when a particular student's tool skill of "writing numbers" never exceeded 40 per minute.

Real-world aims are taken from other students or adults who are required to perform the skill outside the classroom. A good example might be the student who is required to compute without the benefit of a calculator, or even a pencil and paper. It would be important to know the rate or frequency that a student would be expected to calculate in his/her head, in order to be successful on the job.

Reading Aims. The same procedures used in establishing math aims (proficiency standards, intermediate goals, peer performance, tool skills, and real-world applications) are used in reading, as well as other curriculum areas. The following are proficiency standards for reading.

Task Examples	Proficiency Standard Examples
See to Say Sounds	40-60 sounds/min.
See to Say Phonetic Words	40-60 words/min.
Think to Say Alphabet	400 letters/min.
See to Say Letter Names	80-100 letters/min.
See to Say Sight Words	80-100 words/min.
See to Say Words (Orally) in Context	200 words/min.
See to Say Words (Silently) in Context	400 words/min.
Think to Say Facts	15-30 facts/min.

An easy to set initial oral reading aim for primary age students is to double their first trial on passages (e.g., 35 wpm becomes an aim of 70 wpm).

To review, when **selecting a skill** it is important that students are presented with:

- Clear and high expectations
- Consideration for tool (prerequisite) skills
- Skills matching the objectives
- Opportunity to use different Learning Channels.

As you become more confident and comfortable in selecting the skill, the next step (Chapter 3) is providing opportunities for the students to **practice the skill**.

Basic Skill Builders

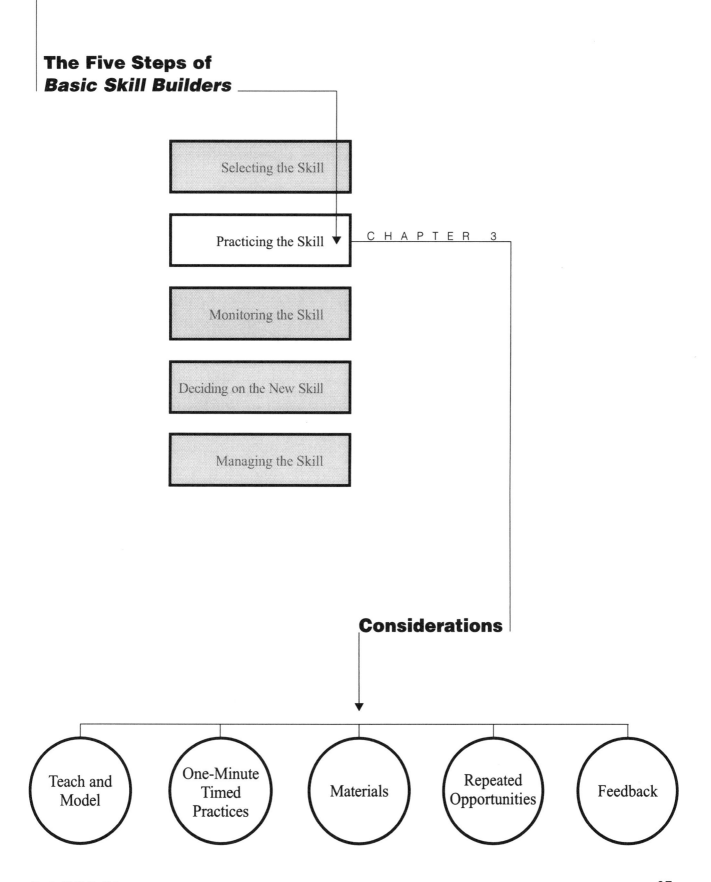

CHAPTER 3

Practicing the Skill

- What is the connection between basic and tool skills?
- How do Learning Channels effect practice?
- What curriculum areas can be practiced with the Skill Builder Sheets?

COMMON TIES BETWEEN THE *BASIC SKILL BUILDERS* MODEL AND THE *EFFECTIVE SCHOOLS RESEARCH*

Here is how *Basic Skill Builders* addresses major points found in the *Effective Schools Research*:

- Time spent on task is the single best predictor of academic success.
- Students are given on task opportunities through repeated one-minute timed practices.
- Students are aware that they will have more than one opportunity to improve their performance.
- Students are more likely to stay on task with one-minute timed practices than during other less organized classroom activities.

THE RELATIONSHIP BETWEEN TOOL SKILLS AND BASIC SKILLS

Before practicing the basic skill (e.g., math, reading, handwriting, etc.), you must first assess the tool skill to ensure that students will grow into the basic skill. A tool skill is the prerequisite skill or the building block for the basic skill. For example, if a student writes a backwards "4" in response to 3 + 1, the problem is the tool skill of writing numbers, not the basic skill of addition. What is a basic skill at one level becomes a tool skill at a more advanced level. For a fifth grader working on the basic skill of long division, there are a number of prerequisite or tool skills necessary: rounding off numbers, estimating, basic multiplication facts, and two- and three-digit subtraction. All of these tool skills were the basic skills at earlier grade levels.

One way for a teacher to experience the impact of tool skills and their relationship to basic skills is to participate in a simple exercise. The activity involves selecting a rudimentary math Skill Builder Sheet, checking the fluency level through a one-minute timed practice, and then repeating the exercise with the non-preferred hand (i.e., if you are right-handed, use your left). For most of us, when we compare the two samples, we immediately find a major difference in the legibility of our responses. Also, we find that we perform at about one-half the speed of our preferred hand. The question is not one of accuracy, but rather of having the tool skill necessary to quickly write numbers. Tool skill deficits can have a profound effect on the success of practicing the basic skill. Building speed and accuracy in the tool skill will help to increase students' speed and accuracy in the basic skills.

Your knowledge of Learning Channels can assist you in assessing content knowledge, even if students lack a specific tool skill. For example, if writing numbers is a tool skill deficit, you might practice the basic skill by using another channel (e.g., See to Say: students look at the math problems and verbally answer).

LEARNING CHANNELS AND THEIR EFFECT ON PRACTICE

When looking for retention and eventual generalization of a skill, Learning Channel practice is a good way to strengthen that skill. Once students reach proficiency on a specific skill, you can look at additional ways to practice the same skill to ensure generalization to other settings. For example, you might begin the practice of two-digit subtraction as a See to Write activity. Once the aim has been met, continue to work on two-digit subtraction, but now change the channel to See to Say, actually a more real life use of the skill of subtraction (e.g., making change, measuring, etc.). The See to Write use of the U.S. Map Skill Builder Sheet, may be changed to a Hear to Write dictation to ensure that students can identify any state in any order in a very short period of time.

Changing the Learning Channel for a particular skill has a variety of uses:

- To capitalize on a channel strength.
- To give opportunity to practice in a deficit channel.
- To provide a variety of practice activities.
- To increase generalization.

OPPORTUNITIES FOR PRACTICE

Basic Skill Builders is guided by timed practices. Pioneers of the Precision Teaching movement discovered that using one-minute timed practices not only aided in the design of practice sheets, but also appeared to provide an interval in which a comfort level could be established. As a result, students could maximize their performance. Anything much longer than several minutes of practice either appeared to bore students, or student performance began to deteriorate.

By keeping the Skill Builder Sheets consistent with a Precision Teaching format, the scoring and recording procedure match the Standard Celeration Chart and the Academic Chart design. The vertical and horizontal axis of these charts are constructed and presented to allow for a visual display of each student's daily number of corrects and errors per minute. Thus, one-minute timed practices are essential in the recording of student performance.

Other things to keep in mind when presenting practice opportunities:

- Promote the value of rate and fluency.
- Keep the material and format consistent.
- Exercise a variety of Learning Channels.
- Set an aim for each skill.
- Consider the tool skill necessary for the basic skill.
- Students should understand the purpose of the timed practice.
- Practice sessions should be at the same time each day.
- Students should manage their own practice sessions.
- Students should self-record and chart immediately following practice.
- Skill Builder Sheets should be challenging, but not cause frustration.
- Acquisition-level tasks should not be practiced without instruction.
- Errors should be considered as opportunities to learn.

USING SKILL BUILDER SHEETS FOR DIFFERENT CURRICULAR AREAS

Skill Builder Sheets and practice can reinforce skills for many different curricular areas, from basic facts in math to vocabulary acquisition in science or social studies, from reading recognition and comprehension to identification of parts of speech, from map identification in geography to government concepts. As teachers examine and use the Skill Builder Sheets available and compare them to the curriculum being taught, they will find that these sheets complement teaching by providing the practice opportunities that students need to become proficient.

The following are examples of some Skill Builder Sheets that you can select for a variety of curricular areas, as well as alternative ways to use them.

CHAPTER 3

Reading. The best way to practice oral reading is to read directly from the text, but there will be instances when it will become necessary to slice back the curriculum to provide practice in some tool skills of oral reading. Always try to keep the task as close to actual classroom activities as possible (e.g., use a Skill Builder Sheet of See to Say phrases first before slicing back to isolated words [see Figures 3-1 and 3-2]).

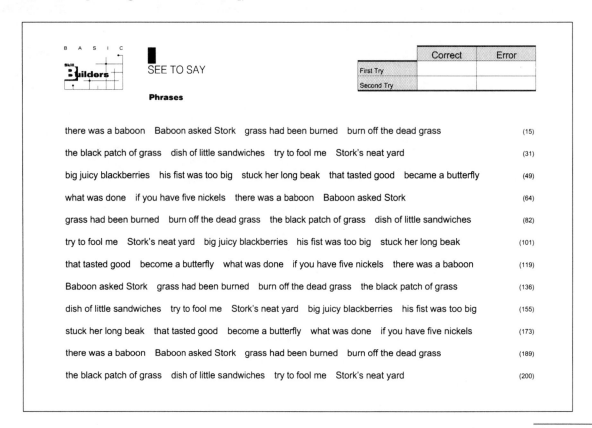

Figure 3-1
See to Say Phrases

SEE TO SAY

Isolated Words

fool	neat	juicy	fist	beak	tasted	neat	fist	fool	juicy	(10)
beak	tasted	fist	fool	juicy	beak	neat	tasted	fist	fool	(20)
beak	juicy	neat	tasted	fist	fool	beak	neat	juicy	tasted	(30)
fist	neat	fool	beak	juicy	tasted	fist	neat	fool	juicy	(40)
beak	tasted	juicy	neat	fool	fist	beak	tasted	fist	fool	(50)
beak	neat	juicy	tasted	fist	fool	beak	neat	juicy	tasted	(60)
fist	fool	beak	neat	juicy	tasted	fist	fool	juicy	neat	(70)
beak	tasted	fist	juicy	neat	beak	tasted	fool	fist	fool	(80)
beak	neat	juicy	tasted	fist	fool	neat	beak	juicy	tasted	(90)
fist	fool	neat	beak	juicy	tasted	fist	fool	neat	juicy	(100)

Figure 3-2
See to Say Isolated Words

In some remedial situations you may use an alternate program with short passages, phrases, and words from word lists (see Figures 3-3, 3-4, and 3-5).

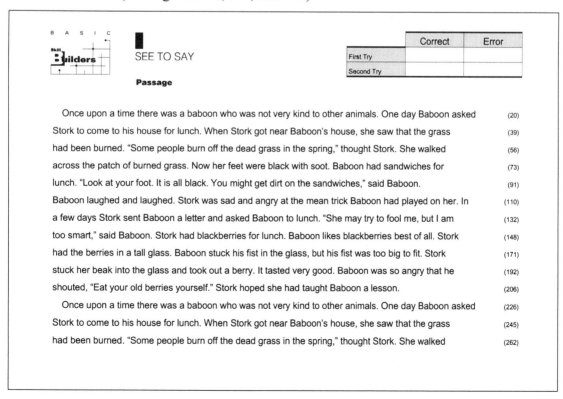

Figure 3-3
See to Say Passage

	Correct	Error
First Try		
Second Try		

Phrases

there was a baboon   Baboon asked Stork   grass had been burned   burn off the dead grass   (15)

the black patch of grass   dish of little sandwiches   try to fool me   Stork's neat yard   (31)

big juicy blackberries   his fist was too big   stuck her long beak   that tasted good   became a butterfly   (49)

what was done   if you have five nickels   there was a baboon   Baboon asked Stork   (64)

grass had been burned   burn off the dead grass   the black patch of grass   dish of little sandwiches   (82)

try to fool me   Stork's neat yard   big juicy blackberries   his fist was too big   stuck her long beak   (101)

that tasted good   become a butterfly   what was done   if you have five nickels   there was a baboon   (119)

Baboon asked Stork   grass had been burned   burn off the dead grass   the black patch of grass   (136)

dish of little sandwiches   try to fool me   Stork's neat yard   big juicy blackberries   his fist was too big   (155)

stuck her long beak   that tasted good   become a butterfly   what was done   if you have five nickels   (173)

there was a baboon   Baboon asked Stork   grass had been burned   burn off the dead grass   (189)

the black patch of grass   dish of little sandwiches   try to fool me   Stork's neat yard   (200)

Figure 3-4
See to Say Phrases

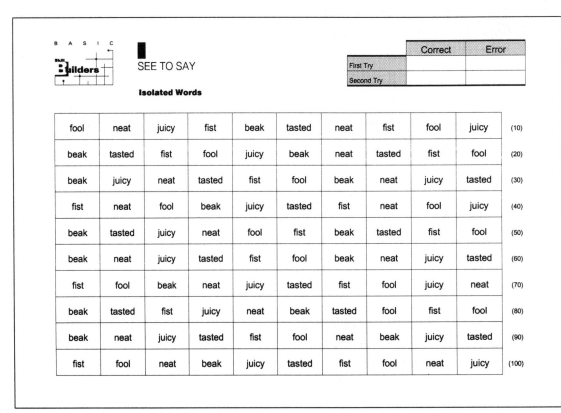

Figure 3-5
See to Say Words

Reading is an area in which you can quickly see a lot of growth. However, since it is a See to Say activity, it does require one student reading at a time. You can do this by using other students, volunteers, or cross-age peers to listen to each student. With students experiencing difficulty in reading, you will want to find time each day to work with these students and use the daily timed practice as the jumping off point for new instruction.

Oral Reading Timings Guidelines

First day of the story:

1. Put the listener's copy of the story under a sheet of acetate.

2. Hand the student his/her folder with a copy of the story. Have the student read for one minute. If the student reaches the bottom of the sheet before the end of one minute, have him/her start over at the top and keep reading.

3. If the student is unable to decode a word immediately, tell the student the word and record it as an error.

4. Record all errors (words mispronounced or provided) by circling the word on the listener's acetate. Do not erase until the next day.

5. Make flash cards of all missed words.

6. Count up all the words read correctly in the one minute and the words missed in the one minute. Ignore the part of the story the student didn't read.

7. Have the student record corrects and errors on the score sheet.

8. Chart, or help the student chart, his/her corrects and errors on the appropriate day line.

9. Set an aim for the student to strive for. Ultimately, the student should be able to read orally at about 200 words per minute. Initially, set an aim that is double the student's first day score.

Following days (rereading exactly the same story passage):

1. Before the story timing, have the student practice the missed words using the flash cards.

2. Do a one-minute warm-up timing using the flash cards. Spread the flash cards out in rows on a table. Have the student read them for one minute.

3. Have the student read the words circled on the listener's acetate once or twice. Do not record this score.

4. Erase the acetate.

5. Then do a timing following all the steps listed for the first day of the story.

Basic Skill Builders

6. After recording/charting the score, compare this day's performance with the performance of the past few days.

If a change is necessary, because of flat data or not enough improvement, decide what you might try. For example:

- Do a one-minute warm-up timing on the first two or three sentences each day before the regular timing. (Don't record this score.)
- Use guided reading as a warm-up for one minute. Read with the student, but read a little bit faster than the student does.
- Use "echo reading." You read a sentence and then the student reads it back to you.

If the student has reached the "aim," move on.

Math. Math Skill Builder Sheets range from basic computation facts and story problems to algebra, geometry, etc. As stated earlier, math is an easy way to begin to use Skill Builder Sheets in the classroom, since most activities can be done by all students at the same time as a See to Write activity. Examples of other kinds of math Skill Builder Sheets include telling time, money, and measurement (see Figures 3-6, 3-7, and 3-8).

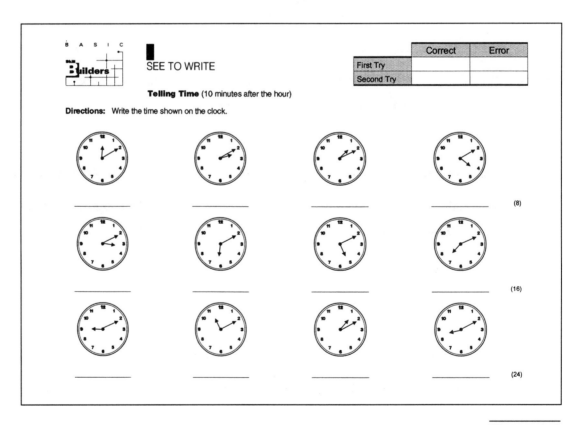

Figure 3-6
Telling Time

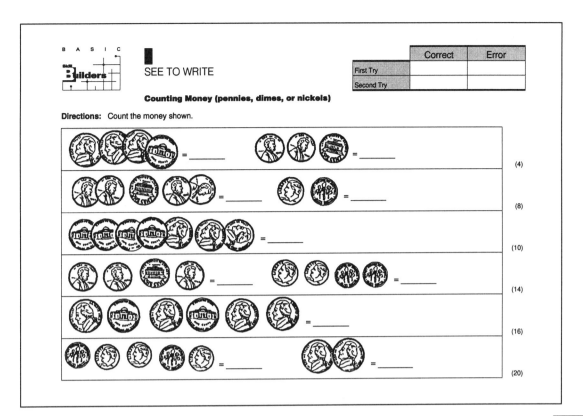

Figure 3-7
Money

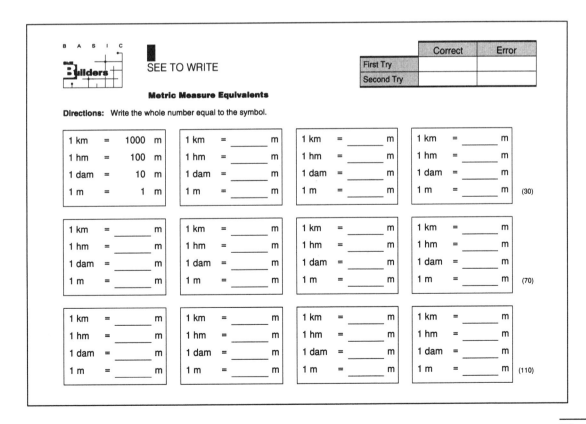

Figure 3-8
Measurement

Dictionary Skills. Alphabetizing and dictionary skills are introduced in many language arts and reading programs, but students often do not get enough practice on the skill during acquisition to become fluent. Skill Builder Sheets can easily provide the practice that students need to make these skills applicable (see Figures 3-9, 3-10, and 3-11).

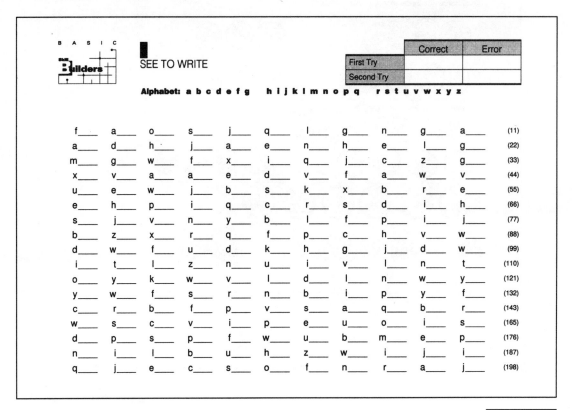

Figure 3-9
Alphabet

BASIC Skill Builders

SEE TO WRITE

Alphabetical Order

	Correct	Error
First Try		
Second Try		

Directions: Does the word come before or after the guide word?

A B C D E F G   H I J K L M N O P Q   R S T U V W X Y Z

fun	___ desk ___	pop	___ off ___	good	___ food ___	new	___ many ___
stole	___ desk ___	not	___ off ___	elf	___ food ___	love	___ many ___
happy	___ desk ___	men	___ off ___	ham	___ food ___	on	___ many ___
pony	___ desk ___	rat	___ off ___	dot	___ food ___	toy	___ many ___
cat	___ desk ___ (5)	queen	___ off ___ (10)	jot	___ food ___ (15)	pat	___ many ___ (20)
ask	___ box ___	luck	___ time ___	top	___ want ___	rip	___ sit ___
cow	___ box ___	sun	___ time ___	you	___ want ___	pet	___ sit ___
am	___ box ___	up	___ time ___	zoo	___ want ___	toy	___ sit ___
eat	___ box ___	zip	___ time ___	ugly	___ want ___	up	___ sit ___
dust	___ box ___ (25)	run	___ time ___ (30)	van	___ want ___ (35)	quit	___ sit ___ (40)
rat	___ pan ___	zoo	___ kick ___	king	___ go ___	fix	___ eye ___
open	___ pan ___	come	___ kick ___	happy	___ go ___	dog	___ eye ___
nose	___ pan ___	stop	___ kick ___	food	___ go ___	gum	___ eye ___
map	___ pan ___	gum	___ kick ___	it	___ go ___	can't	___ eye ___
quit	___ pan ___ (45)	lost	___ kick ___ (50)	jump	___ go ___ (55)	hum	___ eye ___ (60)

Figure 3-10
Alphabetical Order

BASIC Skill Builders

SEE TO WRITE

Guide Words

	Correct	Error
First Try		
Second Try		

Directions: In front of each of these words, put a <u>B</u> if it is before the guide word, <u>S</u> if it is on the same page, and <u>A</u> if it is after the page.

importunate	improbable	breathe	bridle
____ indigo	____ improve	____ bribe	____ brevity
____ inadequacy	____ imperfection	____ bronco	____ breather
____ impolite	____ impose	____ brazen	____ broken
____ impression	____ impound	____ bring	____ bramble
____ implement	____ imprison	____ bracket	____ brief
____ inability	____ impeach	____ bridge	____ breath
	(12)		(24)

bruise	buckle	ape	apology
____ budge	____ buffoon	____ aphid	____ apiary
____ bubble	____ broadcast	____ appearance	____ apoplexy
____ browse	____ bronze	____ antler	____ arbitrary
____ bucket	____ bud	____ apologetics	____ anybody
____ brush	____ buckskin	____ apathy	____ arcade
____ brutal	____ broil	____ aperture	____ apartment
	(36)		(48)

Figure 3-11
Alphabetical Order

CHAPTER 3

Grammar and Word Usage. Practicing the basic skills of identification of parts of speech, subject and verb agreement, capitalization, and use of punctuation marks are easily accomplished through the use of Skill Builder Sheets. When students check their own work it is much easier and more time efficient than assigning pages and pages of grammar homework where you have to correct and grade the results. The following are some examples of Grammar Skill Builder Sheets (see Figures 3-12, 3-13, 3-14, and 3-15).

BASIC Skill Builders

SEE TO MARK

	Correct	Error
First Try		
Second Try		

Nouns in Isolation

keg	strength	skipped	small	whether	school	cabin	silence	(5)
nails	freedom	climbed	peaches	roses	money	wind	has	(11)
came	yacht	with	plan	early	playing	parking	store	(14)
uncle	snow	burned	trimmed	room	desk	picnic	sang	(19)
women	car	feather	town	adventures	class	holiday	died	(26)
seek	doorstep	duty	time	of	club	may	time	(31)
visitors	boys	bravery	mud	coat	settlers	number	to	(38)
why	football	yard	shoes	fire	waiting	delay	before	(43)
paper	box	bought	is	small	captive	opinion	lift	(46)
verb	can	raise	telephone	cat	intermission	hung	horse	(52)
blooming	sentence	were	talking	school	days	Canada	detective	(57)
were	did	college	friend	run	dream	steps	are	(61)
first	subject	teacher	storm	hands	hedge	bandit	children	(68)
garden	section	records	camp	radio	sprang	did	team	(74)
hill	ran	ball	flowers	words	match	gas	diver	(81)
game	pictures	aunt	albums	moved	barn	engine	leader	(88)
brother	medal	group	fight	work	Martha	paw	sand	(96)
cowboy	house	four	stone	how	blanket	fingers	girls	(102)
face	members	street	hit	books	neatly	chair	captain	(108)
city	grass	wall	often	father	man	meadow	mountain	(115)

Figure 3-12
Nouns

SEE TO MARK

Subject Verb Agreement

Directions: Mark the correct verb for each sentence: is/are, was/were, has/have.

There (has, have) been some changes in our plans. Just an hour ago there (was, were) twenty pieces of homemade (2)
candy on that plate. Here (is, are) a new idea for you to use in your essay. There (is, are) room for you. (4)
There (was, were) swordfish, angelfish, and guppies in my friend's new aquarium. There (was, were) eight (6)
puppies in the litter. (There's, There are) some ripe melons on that vine. There (was, were) five homers (8)
hit out of the stadium during the first game of the double-header. There (was, were) not a house in sight. (9)
There (hasn't, haven't) been many customers today because of the heavy snowfall. (There's, There are) only (11)
five shopping days left until Christmas. There (was, were) a fire drill during third period today. There (12)
(is, are) three children sliding down the hill on their sleds. Mr. Prince told us that there (is, are) nine (14)
planets revolving around the sun. For every contestant there (was, were) a prize. (There's, There are) a (16)
man knocking at her front door. The announcer said, "There (is, are) five first prizes, ten second prizes, (17)
fifteen third prizes and twenty fourth prizes in the new magazine contest. (Here's, Here are) the skis for (18)
Jeff. There (has, have) been a delay. (There's, There are) days when I'd like to wring my little brother's (20)
neck. (There's, There are) four letters on the kitchen table that are for you. There (was, were) a better (22)
road up this canyon when I was here last summer. Today (there's, there are) shots for whooping cough, small- (23)
pox, measles, and almost every other disease. There (is, are) an additional charge if we deliver the flowers. (24)
There (is, are) other visitors in the audience from Arizona. On Saturday mornings (there's, there are) usually (26)
four hours of cartoons on television. There (was, were) several answers to the question. There once (27)
(was, were) a small cottage in this grove of pine trees. There (was, were) animal tracks all around the camp. (29)
There (is, are) good program on television on Wednesday evenings. There (was, were) a great deal of excitement (31)
in the halls during Spirit Week. There (is, are) sounds downstairs. (33)

Figure 3-13
Subject Verb Agreement

SEE TO MARK

**Capitals for Special Events, Calendar Items,
Historical Events and Periods, Nationalities, Races, and Religion**

Directions: Mark the letters that need capitals.

The hungarian people have an asiatic background. He is an englishman, but he doesn't (3)
belong to the caucasian race. In New York, columbus day is always a holiday. The (6)
prohibition era was a time of confusion. Jane is reading the chapters on the middle (9)
ages. The battle of the bulge was a decisive event in world war II. Members of the (14)
seventh day adventist church attend services on saturday. thanksgiving is always cele- (19)
brated on thursday. We will celebrate new year's eve by going out to dinner. The (23)
american revolution actually began with the battle of lexington on april 19, 1775. (19)
The fourth of july commemorates the signing of the declaration of independence. Can (32)
you read a french newspaper? christmas this year falls on the fourth wednesday in (35)
december. Where were you on sunday july 10? On july 14, the french celebrate bastille (41)
day. Although Tom attends the presbyterian church, his wife is catholic. The cam- (45)
bodian people have had many hardships. The swedish language is difficult to learn. (46)
Our library has a fine collection of books on buddhism. The NAACP has done much to (47)
improve the civil rights of african americans. On our trip we bought some unusual mexican (50)
pottery. My cousin is a mormon missionary. The bill of rights is a part of the constitution. (54)
The use of tools began in the stone age. My favorite part of american history is (57)
the age of jackson. My visitor is a brazilian. The islam faith has been in the news recently. (61)

Figure 3-14
Capital Letters

Basic Skill Builders

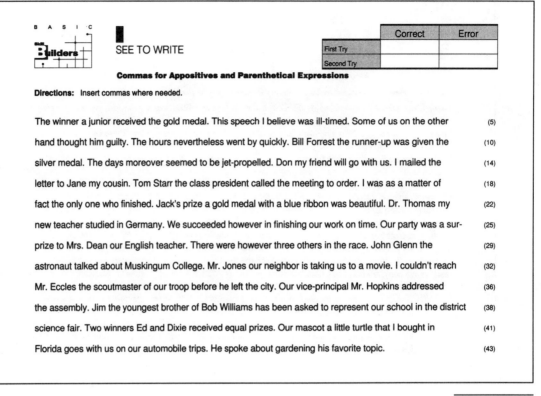

Figure 3-15
Commas

Vocabulary Words, Definitions, and Spelling Words. Vocabulary words and definitions will be specific to the classroom curriculum, but Skill Builder Sheets can be developed to provide additional practice in these skills. There are some considerations to remember when developing your own skill sheets:

- Consistent format—use one similar to commercial Skill Builder Sheets.
- Place words or definitions left to right on the page.
- Put a cumulative count at the end of each row.
- Provide more items or problems on the page than can be completed in one minute.
- Repeat new items or problems over and over on same page.
- Space the items or problems to permit ample answer space.
- Randomly distribute the items or problems on page.
- Skill activity must relate directly to the tool or basic skill.

The following are some examples of teacher-generated Skill Builder Sheets that are specific to certain curriculum areas (see Figures 3-16, 3-17, and 3-18).

Skill Sheet

Vocabulary: Constitution

impeach   safegards   dominate   amended   unconstitutional   convention   foundation   constitution   1789

control, take over _____	when constitution was ratified _____ (12)
protection _____	charge with wrong doing _____ (29)
going against the constitution _____	a base _____ (55)
when constitution was ratifed _____	control, take over _____ (67)
charge with wrong doing _____	protection _____ (84)
7 articles establishing government _____	a base _____ (106)
a base _____	7 articles establishing government _____ (128)
changed _____	meeting, assembly _____ (145)
when constitution was ratified _____	charge with wrong doing _____ (156)
protection _____	going against the constitution _____ (182)
control, take over _____	changed _____ (197)
charge with wrong doing _____	protection _____ (214)
7 articles establishing government _____	a base _____ (236)
meeting, assembly _____	when constitution was ratified _____ (250)
when constitution was ratified _____	charge with wrong doing _____ (261)
changed _____	meeting, assembly _____ (278)
going against the constitution _____	changed _____ (301)
meeting, assembly _____	control, take over _____ (319)
a base _____	going against the constitution _____ (341)

Figure 3-16
Vocabulary

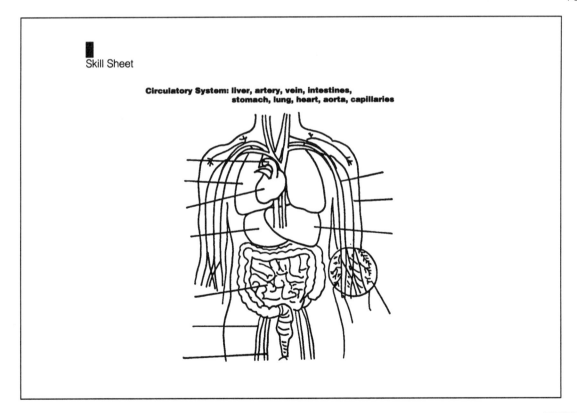

Figure 3-17
Circulatory System

Basic Skill Builders

Skill Sheet

Vocabulary

Directions: Circle the correctly spelled word in each group. Write the word correctly.

lend	wrene	perne	slender	tracter	celler
lende	wren	penney	slendor	tractor	cellor
leche	ren	penny	slendar	tractar	cellar

_____ _____ _____ _____ _____ _____ (12)

pebble	levle	petle	bench	wrensh	plentey
pebbel	level	petel	bensh	wrench	plenty
pebbal	leval	petal	benche	rench	plente

_____ _____ _____ _____ _____ _____ (24)

clever	splender	necter	freckle	reble	medle
clevor	splendor	nector	freckel	rebel	medel
clevar	splendar	nectar	freckal	rebal	medal

_____ _____ _____ _____ _____ _____ (36)

themselves	neaglect	telagram	project	elament	sprede
themselfs	neglect	telelgrame	progect	element	spred
thenselves	neglekt	telegram	projekt	elument	spread

_____ _____ _____ _____ _____ _____ (48)

Figure 3-18
Spelling

Once the skill has been selected and ample practice opportunities have been provided, the next step is to monitor the skill. Chapter 4 will discuss why and how to monitor progress.

The Five Steps of
Basic Skill Builders

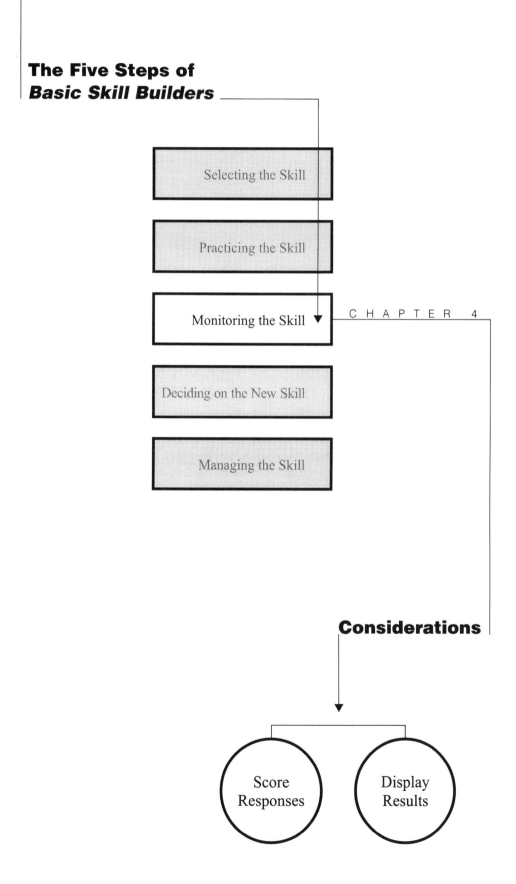

CHAPTER 4

Considerations

CHAPTER 4

Monitoring the Skill

- Why monitor?
- What is common to *Basic Skill Builders* and *Effective Schools Research*?
- What makes for good monitoring?
- What methods are best to visually display and interpret student data?

MONITORING PERFORMANCE

The most compelling argument for monitoring student performance is in the use of data to make more informed instructional and curricular decisions. By keeping track of performance, you, and more importantly the students, can see where they have been, where they are now, and where they might be in the future. This continuous monitoring allows us to analyze the past, examine the present, and predict the future. As a by-product, the students have the benefit of immediate feedback and a continual visual display of their progress.

The *Basic Skill Builders* model embraces a system of measurement in which using daily one-minute timed practices permits teachers and students to make on-the-spot decisions regarding the appropriateness of the skill sheets, and the extent to which instructional or curricular changes should be made.

COMMON TIES BETWEEN THE *BASIC SKILL BUILDERS* MODEL AND THE *EFFECTIVE SCHOOLS RESEARCH*

The following outlines what is common to both *Basic Skill Builders* and the *Effective Schools Research*:

- Student performance is continually monitored.
- Students receive immediate feedback.

- Measurement (monitoring) is directly aligned with the student task and the instructional objective.
- Students maintain a visual display of their performance.
- Teachers monitor results of decision making.

EFFECTIVE MONITORING

Two ingredients comprise effective monitoring. The first is that the measurement must be direct. If students are required to demonstrate a basic skill by working in a district-adopted workbook, they should be measured by using exercises either from that workbook or exercises that are closely related. Unfortunately, student performance is often indirectly measured by using standardized tests that are not congruent with the demands of the district curriculum. It is the authors' belief that it is far more appropriate and fair to monitor student performance by measuring from the day-to-day curriculum.

The second requirement of effective monitoring is that it be continuous. Daily measurement permits immediate feedback to students, and also allows a visual display of each student's learning and progress. By obtaining daily performance statements and monitoring changes in the performance, learning is obvious and visual patterns begin to emerge.

Traditional measurement usually requires that students take an end-of-chapter test or some type of pre-posttest where they are measured at the beginning of the year or unit, and then again at the end. Unfortunately, a lot of "water has passed under the bridge" between the point of instruction and the measurement. As Ogden R. Lindsley once said, "We use pre-posttests to see how we have done, we use continuous measurement to see how we are doing." Teachers simply lose valuable instructional time and face more remediation and reteaching with traditional measurement practices. In Chapter 5 we will examine how daily monitoring leads to more precise methods in making instructional and curricular decisions.

To summarize, *Basic Skill Builders* incorporates both **direct** and **continuous** monitoring in its process; direct in that the measurement comes directly from student curriculum, and continuous in that it is enacted daily. Together these concepts form the basis for better instructional and curricular decision making.

TRACKING STUDENT PERFORMANCE

From the *Effective Schools Research* we have learned that students are more likely to improve their performance if a graphic display is available. Most of the time students prefer keeping their records to themselves, however, there are times when public posting is more appropriate. In the authors' experience, primary and intermediate level students seem to take pride in public posting, while many middle and high school students prefer individual charting. In either case, the most important consideration has to do with tracking daily performance, providing immediate feedback, and analyzing the data.

Several options exist for tracking students' daily scores. The first is a simple scoring sheet (see Figure 4-1) where the date is posted, the specific Skill Builder Sheet is listed, and the correct and error counts are recorded. This procedure is the most basic of the options, and offers students the opportunity to directly view their progress across time.

Date	*Skill Sheet*	*Correct*	*Error*
10/15	Add Facts (0-10)	65	5
10/16	Add Facts (0-10)	70	2
10/17	Add Facts (0-10)	75	1
10/18	Add Facts (11-18)	63	2
10/19	Add Facts (11-18)	68	2
10/22	Add Facts (11-18)	72	1
10/23	Add Facts (11-18)	74	1

Figure 4-1
Daily Record Sheet

A somewhat better tracking option is to provide a picture of the scores by using a graph common in most classrooms. Figure 4-2 is an Equal Interval Graph showing the days of the week (Monday-Friday) across the bottom (horizontal axis), and the number of corrects and errors along the left-hand scale (vertical axis). Note that the distance between the days-of-the-week lines and the count lines is equal. The intervals between 10 and 20, 20 and 30, etc. are the same, thus the Equal Interval Graph.

In the following example, correct responses are represented by dots while errors are represented by Xs. The example shows that on Tuesday the student had 65 corrects and 5 errors, Wednesday 70 correct and 2 errors, and Thursday 75 correct and 1 error.

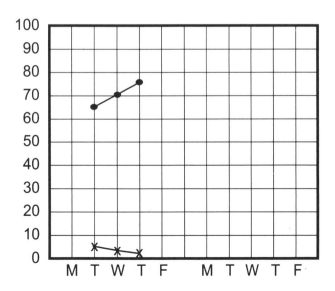

Figure 4-2
Equal Interval Graph

Basic Skill Builders   59

CHAPTER 4

The third and most accurate tracking option is using the Standard Celeration Chart (see Figure 4-3). At first this chart seems somewhat overwhelming, however, with practice and use it will become a tool that not only tracks students, but allows you to be much more precise when making instructional and curricular decisions.

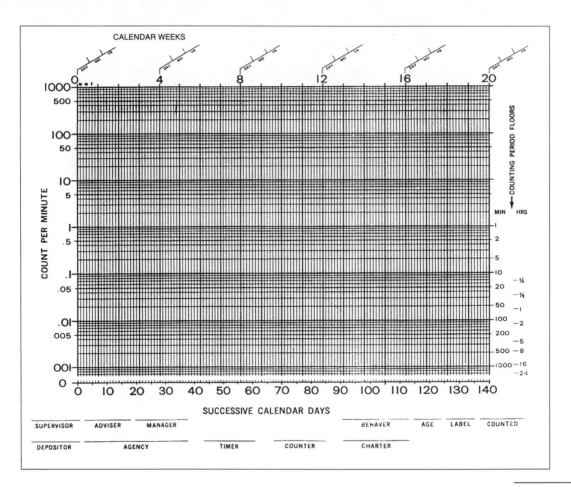

Figure 4-3
Standard Celeration Chart

Properties of the Standard Celeration Chart

1. This semi-logarithmic design has a vertical axis (left-hand side) displaying count per minute on the logarithmic scale. The horizontal axis (bottom side) represents the days of the week and has equal distances between lines—thus, **semi**-logarithmic.

2. Performance records can be maintained for behavior that occurs as infrequently as once in a 24-hour period, to as frequently as 1,000 times per minute.

3. Student performance data can be tracked for 140 days or 20 weeks on a single piece of paper. These numbers represent about one semester of school, which entails using two pieces of chart paper per student per year.

4. Performance data can be analyzed and interpreted using proportional growth statements. The advantage is that students of different abilities can be viewed as growing against themselves, as opposed to others. For example, student "A" (see Figure 4-4) with performance scores that change from 10 to 20 has the same 100% growth statement as student "B" has who grows from 40 to 80 in the same period. Further, when drawing a best-fit line through the data points, there is an identical slope or angle to the data set. This is not the case when viewing the same data on a traditional equal interval graph. In the example below we see the same proportional growth in both displays, however, when inspecting the slope or angle of growth on the Equal Interval Graph there appears to be a more noticeable difference. Keep in mind that both students ("A" and "B") demonstrate proportionally the same growth.

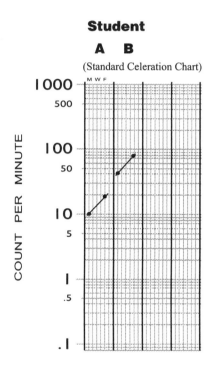
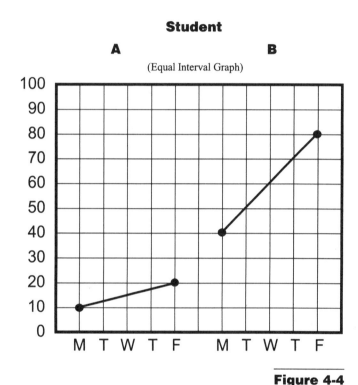

Figure 4-4
Using Different Growth Displays

Properties of the Academic Chart

1. The major difference between the Standard Celeration Chart (SCC) and the Academic Chart is that the latter only uses the top half (1 to 1,000) of the SCC. The Academic Chart (see Figure 4-5) provides the advantage of recording raw scores should there not be the opportunity to record on the chart itself. The Academic Chart more closely fits with the Skill Builder Sheets and the one-minute timed practices.

CHAPTER 4

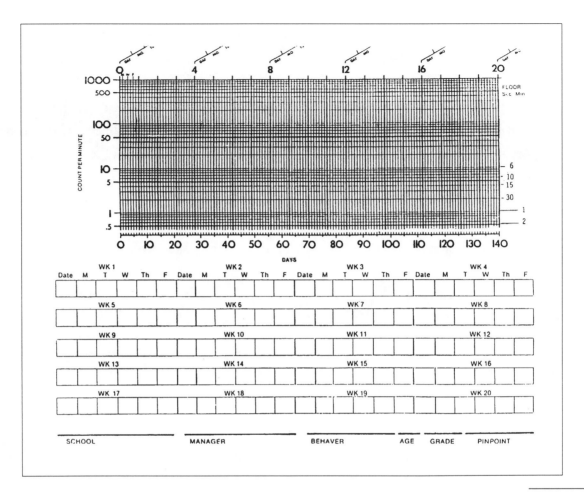

Figure 4-5
Academic Chart

Recording and Charting Procedures

1. The first step in getting dots on the chart is to score each student's work and record the raw data on some type of form. This could be as simple as listing the days of the week and recording the number of corrects and errors next to the corresponding day.

   Keep in mind that scores are converted to the number of correct and incorrect responses per minute. Since the timed practices are one minute in duration, converting should not be a problem. However, where one minute is not the common denominator, merely divide the number of responses (correct and errors) by the interval of time. For example if a student recorded 100 responses in two minutes, the data would be converted to a statement of 50 per minute. On the other hand, if a student scored 50 correct in 30 seconds, the data would be converted to 100 per minute. Scores are recorded as such when using either the Standard Celeration or the Academic Chart.

2. After the data are converted to count per minute, you or the student can use a #2 pencil to record the scores by making dots on the chart. To keep things standard use dots to represent corrects and xs to show errors or incorrects. To record, locate and mark where the day line intersects the count-per-minute line. Day lines and scores from 1 to 10 are easy to find and mark. The teacher merely finds the day (Monday-Friday) and then locates the frequency or rate lines. For those scores between 10 and 1000, there is a bit of estimating required.

   Note that on Figure 4-6 the score of 15 is marked about half-way between the 10 and 20 lines. A score of 35 would be recorded about half-way between the 30 and 40 lines.

3. Now that the data have been recorded on the chart, the next thing is to connect all the dots within one calendar week. The heavy lines represent Sundays. Data points between Monday and Friday of each week should be connected (see Figure 4-6).

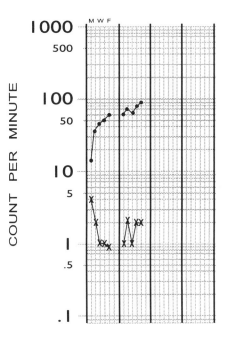

Figure 4-6
Dropping the Dots

CHAPTER 4

Charting Practice

The following Figure 4-7 is an opportunity for you to practice by taking three weeks of student performance and charting the scores. Use dots for correct responses and xs for errors. You can check your charting skills by using the answer key at the end of this chapter.

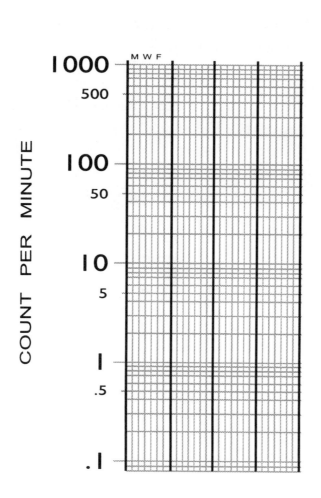

Week 1		
	Corrects	Errors
M	10	2
T	60	5
W	80	8
Th	30	7
F	90	1
Week 2		
	Corrects	Errors
M	100	10
T	500	8
W	400	6
Th	700	3
F	1,000	2
Week 3		
	Corrects	Errors
M	10	3
T	20	2
W	15	1
Th	37	0
F	82	0

Figure 4-7
Charting Exercise

4. Two other charting procedures that should be considered have to do with **aims** and **phase changes**. For review, aims are established to help students work toward an expectation. Sometimes the aims are the same as the Proficiency Standards, however, in some instances aims are considered an intermediate goal. In either case aims are indicated on the chart by drawing an "A" at the level of expectation. In Figure 4-8 the aim has been set at 70 per minute.

The second charting practice deals with the procedure of indicating when you or the students make an instructional or curricular change. Notice in Figure 4-8 the vertical and horizontal lines indicating the decision to move from one Skill Builder Sheet ("Add Facts 0-10") to another ("Add Facts 11-18").

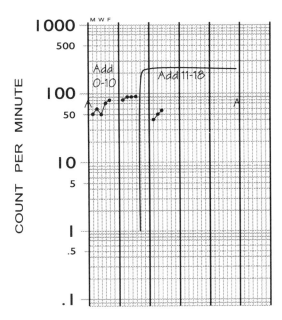

Figure 4-8
Aims and Phase Changes

5. The beauty of direct and continuous measurement is the opportunity it provides to review students' past performances in relationship to their current level of functioning. To some extent the data may also help predict future performance.

One of the last steps in charting rests in the analysis of the data. Several things must occur when examining data:

- Determine whether the daily scores are growing, maintaining, or worsening. This can be done by visually estimating or following the rule of the **best-fit line**. In the latter case, a line is drawn through the set of data that best reflects the angle or slope of the scores (see Figure 4-9) and roughly displays half the dots below and half above the line.

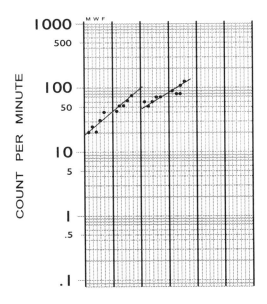

Figure 4-9
Best-Fit Line

Basic Skill Builders

- Next, the slope or direction of the data are quantified by using a procedure to determine a **celeration statement**. Celeration, in *Basic Skill Builders*' language, means the extent to which the performance changed from one week to the next, or from one set of scores to the next. The change is expressed as a **times** (x) if the responses are increasing or accelerating, and a **divide** (÷) if the data show a decrease or deceleration.

To calculate celeration statements use a mathematical formula of dividing the median score of one set of scores into the median of a second set of scores. For example, if the median of week one was 20 and the median of week two was 30, the celeration statement would be read as (times) x 1.50 and be interpreted as a 50% growth from the first to second week. The same process would be used if a set of scores covering several weeks was divided into a second set of scores (30 ÷ 20 = x 1.50).

Furthermore, if the median of the first week was 60 and the second week was 40, you would divide the smaller value into the larger. However, in this example the data show a **decline**, so the celeration statement would be read as (divide by) ÷ 1.50 (60 ÷ 40 = ÷ 1.50).

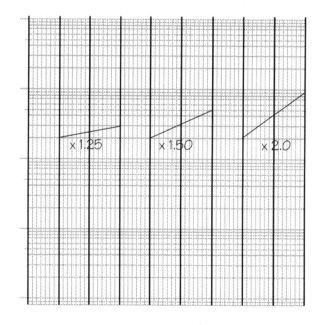

Figure 4-10
Celerations and Slopes

The history of *Basic Skill Builders* has led us to believe that students who engage in appropriate practice should grow a minimum of X 1.25 or 25% a week. One way of determining if there is at least a 25% growth is to estimate the slope of the line by examining and becoming familiar with what various slopes and their angles look like. Figure 4-10 represents different slopes and their percentage of growth.

Experience has shown that using the best-fit line to determine whether the student is growing at least 25% a week is the easiest way to decide whether a change of instruction is in order. Chapter 5 investigates more about instructional and curricular decision making and the alternatives.

Finally, the important aspects to remember about monitoring students are that they need to be:

- Directly monitored from the curriculum.
- Continually monitored.
- Given immediate feedback.
- Presented with a visual display of their progress.

The authors suggest the use of the Academic Chart for monitoring because it maintains a standard format that provides:

- A view of the past, present, and future.
- A visual display of performance and learning.
- A statement of proportional growth.
- A visual of the slope and the degree of learning.

The next step is taking the performance of students and deciding whether an instructional or curricular change is needed, as well as what to do when a change is indicated. These concepts will be addressed in Chapter 5.

Answer Key. Earlier in this chapter a charting exercise (see Figure 4-7) was presented that required you to take raw student data and chart the corrects and errors. Compare your answers with the key presented in Figure 4-11.

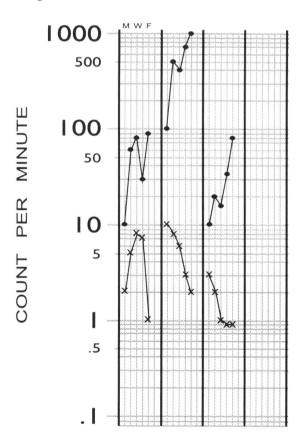

Figure 4-11
Charting Answer Key

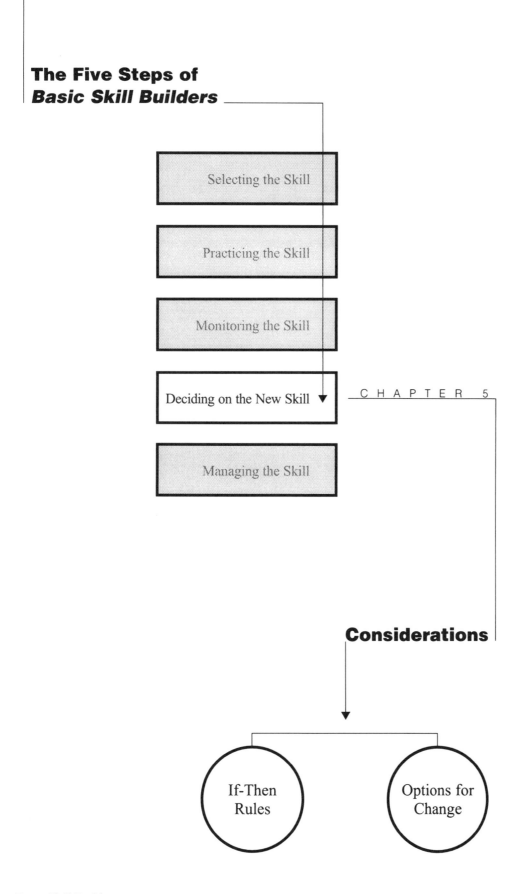

CHAPTER 5

Deciding on the New Skill

- What are some indications of when a change is needed?
- What kind of changes should be made?
- What should be done when learning has stalled?

INTRODUCTION

The last and possibly most important step in the *Basic Skill Builders* process is that of using the data collected during the practice and monitoring stages (Chapters 3 and 4) to **make instructional and curricular decisions**. By looking at the recorded scores occurring over a period of a week or two, teachers, parents, or students can quickly decide if:

- The students have reached a high degree of excellence or proficiency on the skill, and it is now time to move on to a more challenging skill; or
- The students are not learning the selected skill quickly enough, and some additional instructional intervention is needed; or
- The students are learning the skill but have not yet reached proficiency, so they should continue to practice.

COMMON TIES BETWEEN THE *BASIC SKILL BUILDERS* MODEL AND THE *EFFECTIVE SCHOOLS RESEARCH*

The following is what the *Effective Schools Research* and *Basic Skill Builders* promote when using student performance data to make decisions:

- Results are used not only to evaluate students but also for instructional diagnosis, and to find out if teaching methods are working.
- Deciding that a skill or concept has been mastered is based on standards set high enough to promote excellence.
- Parents should also be encouraged to keep track of student progress.
- Rather than making comparisons with other students, a student's learning should be compared with his/her own past performance.

INDICATIONS OF A NEEDED CHANGE

To maximize academic achievement, students cannot waste time practicing skills they find too easy, or skills in which they have already reached fluency. Nor can they afford the wasted time and frustration that occur when they "spin their wheels" practicing a skill in a manner that does not result in increased performance or learning. To determine when it is time to move on or time to intervene, the recorded data should be frequently and regularly reviewed at least once a week. The decision to change is based on the following rules:

- **At Aim for Two Days**

    If a student's scores (the number of correct responses per minute) are at or above the previously set aim or goal, it is time for a change. To ensure that scores are valid, students are typically expected to demonstrate proficient performance more than once. For example in Figure 5-1, the aim for reading Dolch Words was set at 100 words correct per minute. The student's scores over four days were 94, 103, 97, and 102. Two of the last three scores have been at aim (103, 102), suggesting that the student is ready for a more difficult task.

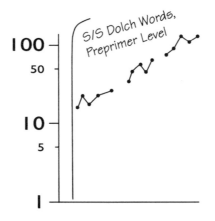

Figure 5-1
At Aim

- **Three Days of Flat Data**

    It is possible that students might stop making progress before reaching the set aim. In Figure 5-2, learning was occurring because the scores were generally increasing. However, the scores for the last days (50, 51, 49) have "flattened out" and suggest that learning has stalled. Once students have three consecutive days of this kind of "flat data," it is unlikely that further increases in performance will occur without some kind of instructional intervention to reactivate the learning.

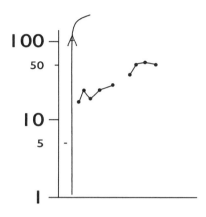

Figure 5-2
Flat Data

- **Less than 25% Growth Each Week**

Learning may be occurring, but at such a minimal level that we cannot expect students to reach their aims in any reasonable number of days. The scores for the past two weeks in Figure 5-3 are generally increasing, but the increase is barely noticeable.

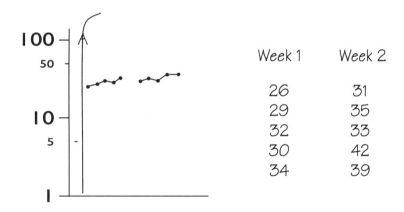

Figure 5-3
Insufficient Growth

Experience has suggested that we should see at least 25% growth from one week to the next. Whether or not 25% growth has occurred over the past two weeks can be determined by one of several methods:

- Divide the median (middle score) of week one into the median of week two. In Figure 5-3 the median of week one was 30 and the median of week two was 35; the celeration would be x 1.16 (35 ÷ 30 = 1.16) or 16% growth, which is less than the required minimum of 25%.

Basic Skill Builders

Examine the charted data. Draw a best-fit line through the data that best reflects the angle or slope of the past two weeks. The line should show half the dots below and half above. A simple approach is to lay a standard size pencil across the data so that all the dots are covered. The pencil will reflect the slope of the data (see Figure 5-4).

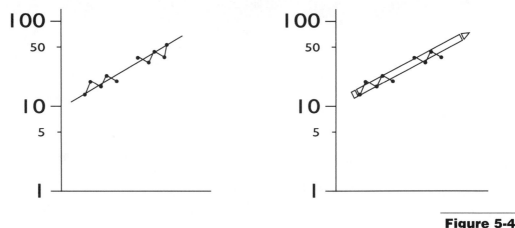

Figure 5-4
Best-Fit Line and Using a Pencil

On an Academic or Standard Celeration Chart, 25% growth is reflected by the slope pictured in Figure 5-5. Compare the slope of the best-fit line or the pencil on the chart (see Figure 5-4) with the reference slope (see Figure 5-5) and estimate whether students are progressing at more or less than 25% per week. If less than 25% growth is occurring, some intervention is needed.

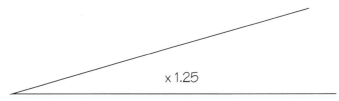

Figure 5-5
25% Growth Reference Slope

DECIDING WHAT KIND OF CHANGES SHOULD BE MADE

If students have not reached their aims, and the data for the last three days have not flattened out, and the correct scores show at least 25% growth, **then** none of the aforementioned rules apply and students should continue practicing the skill in the same manner until reaching their aims. However, if the rules suggest the need for a change, the next step is to decide what specific change should be made. This decision will depend on several factors including the level or stage of skill development at which students may be operating, with respect to the selected skill.

When learning a new skill, students typically move through a series of specific skill development levels or stages, including the three presented in Figure 5-6.

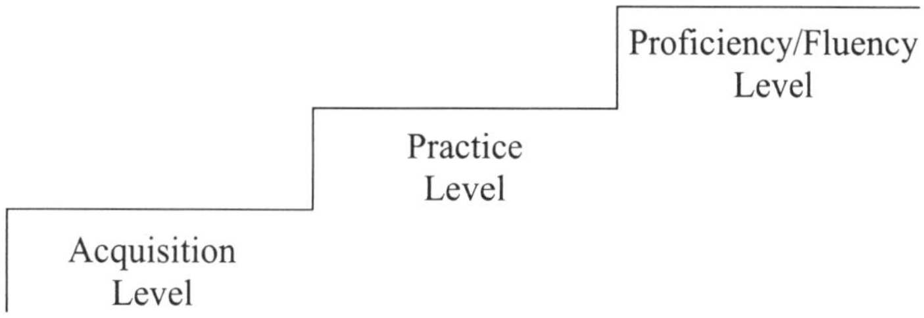

Figure 5-6
Levels of Skill Development

Acquisition Level. In the acquisition level students are learning how to correctly respond to a new skill. They are acquiring a new skill, so in depth practice of that skill is imperative. Timed practices should not replace instruction but can be used to monitor the effectiveness of the teaching techniques. Students are probably functioning at the acquisition level if the recorded data indicate:

- Correct responses occurring at a low rate (e.g., less than 20 correct per minute).
- A lot of inconsistent errors.
- A lot of up and down variation in scores from day to day.

If a change is needed and students are performing at the acquisition level, consider:

- Providing more direct instruction on the skill.
- Working on tool skills along with or instead of the current skill.
- Changing Learning Channels to one that is easier for students.
- Providing more frequent feedback, possibly even reinforcing each response.

Practice Level. In the practice level students are refining a skill they have previously acquired. They are becoming more accurate, as well as increasing their rate of response. It is at this level that students would be working toward mastery of a skill. Students are functioning at the practice level if the recorded data indicate:

- Correct responses at a middle frequency level (e.g., more than 20 per minute, but less than the proficiency aim).
- Errors occurring at a low frequency level (e.g., less than five errors per minute).
- Less up and down variation in the scores from day to day.

If a change is necessary when the student is performing at this level, consider:

- Providing less overall instruction, but providing instruction specifically addressing the errors made.
- Providing a lot of short, repeated practice opportunities.
- Keeping the Learning Channel consistent from day to day, unless a channel change is necessary to facilitate growth.

Proficiency or Fluency Level. At this level, students are strengthening their command of the skill. A proficient learner can demonstrate both accuracy **and** speed. For example, proficient performance is the difference between knowing how to type accurately but slowly, and being a competent typist. The skill has become automatic and can now be generalized and applied to other, more complex situations.

Students are functioning at proficient or fluent level if the recorded data and observed performance indicate:

- High correct frequencies at or near the performance standard or aim.
- Few, if any, errors.
- Little up and down variation in scores.
- Smooth, easy, rhythmic responding.

If students have reached the aim frequency and can perform the skill proficiently, it is clearly time for a change to a more difficult task. The change might reflect a small step forward in the curriculum, such as changing from the task of "Add Facts Sums to 10" to the task of "Add Facts Sums to 11." It may reflect a larger step, such as changing from "Add Facts Sums to 18" to "Subtract Facts Sums to 18." Whatever the new task, it should **add on** enough curriculum weight that students' initial performances drop back down into the acquisition or practice range. Figure 5-7 demonstrates this phenomenon.

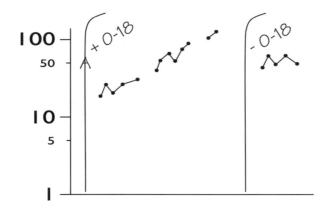

Figure 5-7
"Add On" Curriculum

The data presented in Figure 5-8 illustrate that the new tasks selected are too easy. The example student is being given new tasks on which he/she is already or almost at aim. Already proficient on these small skills, the student is wasting valuable practice and learning time. The example student ought to be taking bigger leaps forward through the curriculum. A more appropriate computation task might be to ask the student to "Add Facts Sums to 18."

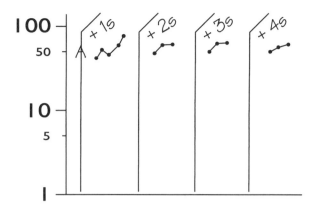

Figure 5-8
Task Is Too Easy

STALLED LEARNING

If the data reflect a lack of acceptable growth or learning before students reach aim, it is important to intervene with some additional support. The following are several different skill building options that will help.

Provide More Practice Before or During the Skill Builder Timed Practices

- Implement multiple timed practices. Complete the Skill Builder Sheets timed practices more than once and only record the best score.
- Provide extra opportunities for practice. Set up a center where students can do additional timed practices during their free time.
- Provide untimed practice activities. Use games, flash cards, computer activities, etc. that relate to the selected skill.
- Do paired timings. Pair or precede the timed practices on the selected skill with practices on related skills for a warm-up:
    - A related tool skill (e.g., writing numbers 0-9 before multiplication facts 0-9).
    - A section or portion of the selected task (e.g., practice new vocabulary words before reading an oral passage).
    - Learning opportunities or errors; practice items missed during the last practice before the day's regular timed practice.
    - A different Learning Channel (e.g., read a math Skill Builder Sheet aloud [See to Say] before the written [See to Write] timed practice that will be recorded).
- Use a pacing tape, a metronome, or another pacing device and set the frequency at the level at which students should perform.
- Use a Skill Builder Sheet with answers at the top for students to use as a reference.
- Have students switch to a different Learning Channel that is easier for them.

Basic Skill Builders

- Slice back the selected task for an easier, but related one (e.g., identifying just the Western States rather than all fifty).

Use Motivational Tactics

- Provide immediate feedback. Review students' charts or scores as soon as the timings are finished.
- Set aims a day or week at a time.
- Use behavior contracts to have students predict when aims will be reached or what weekly growth will be attained and then reward those accomplishments.
- Use incentives programs (e.g., if better today than yesterday, student receives a reward).

FINAL THOUGHT

There is no one right answer or change. The decision "rules" (discussed at the beginning of this chapter) indicate when a new task or intervention is needed. The actual option selected will depend on the student, the teachers, the curricula, the previously selected skills, the skill development levels observed, etc.

What is important is that when a change is indicated, students, parents, and teachers take their best guess and enact some sort of change. Continued practice and monitoring through the use of one-minute timed practices on the new skill or under the new instructional conditions will result in new data being analyzed. If acceptable growth is observed, great! The decision was a good one. If after a week's time, no or insufficient improvement is observed in the recorded scores, another change can be made. The final "rule" is to use the data to monitor success and, if necessary, **try, try again**!

The Five Steps of *Basic Skill Builders*

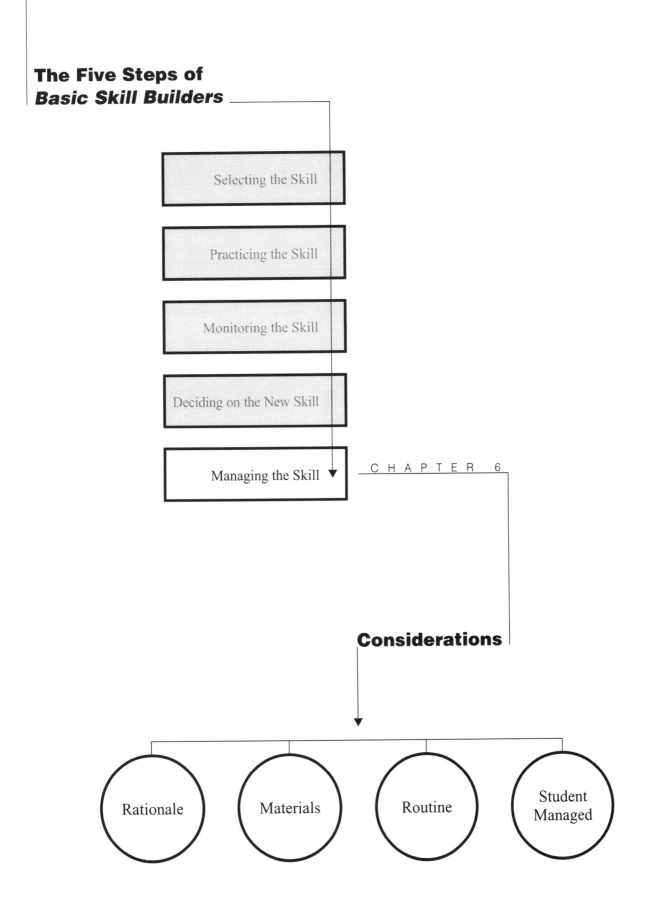

CHAPTER 6

Considerations

- Rationale
- Materials
- Routine
- Student Managed

CHAPTER 6

Managing the Skill

- What are the steps to take before classroom implementation?
- What are the necessary materials?
- What are the steps involved in classroom organization?

When implementing the *Basic Skill Builders* model, keep in mind the elements reviewed in earlier chapters. You must select the appropriate skill, provide students with many opportunities to practice, monitor their performance, and finally make decisions from the data. How do you, as the teacher, manage all of this with 30 students and the everyday demands of the classroom? The answer lies not so much in having to "add" something new, but rather how can the concept of *Basic Skill Builders* blend into what is already going on in your classroom.

If used as a routine in the regular classroom, the practice sessions, scoring, and recording should take no longer than about 15-20 minutes per day. With special education teachers, the practice sessions, as well as recording performance, will require a little more time. In fact, special education resource room teachers may find the Skill Builder Sheets very useful, not only for reinforcing the regular curriculum, but as a major part of their daily classroom routine.

STEPS BEFORE CLASSROOM IMPLEMENTATION

Administrator. The first step should be to get support from the building administration. Any new idea, program, project, model, etc. should have administrative approval and support from the outset. With administrative endorsement, there is a greater chance of success. So, the first thing to do is discuss and demonstrate the *Basic Skill Builder* process with the building leadership. The following are some suggestions to help build support.

Explain the concept by emphasizing how many of the classroom practices found in the *Effective Schools Research* reflect the *Basic Skill Builders* model. Discuss the importance of setting clear and high expectations, providing a sequential curriculum in a visually consistent format, and offering students frequent opportunities to practice. Reinforce how tracking performance on a daily basis leads to better instructional and curricular decisions. Review the *Basic Skill Builders* research by pointing out that it has been approved and validated by the U.S. Department of Education for use in both special and regular education. In addition, longitudinal studies (Great Falls, Montana Public Schools) support that students under the model of "building skills to proficiency":

- Maintain the skill over time.
- Are able to advance more quickly to other skills.
- Generalize the skill across settings.

Clarify that *Basic Skill Builders* will not replace current curriculum, but rather reinforce it by providing practice. The practice sessions should not take more than 15-20 minutes per day. Finally, suggest that not only will there be significant growth in basic skills, but students will be excited by the one-minute timed practices and the opportunity to track their daily progress with a graphic display.

Teachers. When establishing the groundwork with teachers, introduce the *Basic Skill Builders* model in much the same way that you did with administrators. After presenting the overall philosophy, have teachers take a series of one-minute timed practices to get a feel for them and the effect they have on learning a new skill. It is also suggested that you use something like a U.S. Map Skill Builder Sheet and have teachers identify states. Colleagues could have the opportunity to observe individual growth over three timings. When describing the model, include the important elements of expectations, fluency, curriculum format, charting, and decision making. It will also be helpful to share some examples of other Skill Builder Sheets. The map Skill Builder Sheets are usually effective in illustrating the idea behind curriculum slicing, consistent format, and monitoring performance from a large portion of the curricula.

Students. Students tend to readily adapt to the *Basic Skill Builders* model because they like the idea of having:

- Clear expectations.
- High expectations.
- The curriculum presented in visually consistent format.
- The teacher demonstrating, then doing it together, then doing it independently.
- The opportunity for repeated practice using one-minute Skill Builder Sheets.
- Immediate feedback and a visual display of their performance.
- Incentives and rewards for learning.

When explaining the model in detail to students, explain:

- Why proficiency is important.
- How to reach proficiency through one-minute timed practices.
- How to score and record performances.
- How they can help in curricular decisions.

Parents. Parents often play a significant role in reinforcing what happens in the classroom. In that regard, it is highly effective to prepare packets and send them home. Once again, your approach is similar to when you explained the merits of the model to the building administrator and other teachers. Point out that there is good reason to believe that practice leads to proficiency, and proficiency means the students have command of the skills. Furthermore, when students have command of skills, they maintain them over time, can transfer them to more complex tasks, and are able to generalize the skills to other academic and real-world settings.

With a little coaching, parents can help select Skill Builder Sheets, administer one-minute timed practices, help score and chart student performance, and perhaps as important as anything, offer rewards and incentives at home.

ORGANIZATIONAL SUGGESTIONS FOR GETTING STARTED

Once teachers decide if this will be a class-wide implementation, or only for selected individuals, they can move ahead with how it will be managed. For example, if the entire class will participate in one-minute timed practices, then a specific time is reserved each day for sessions, a routine is established for the distribution of student folders, a procedure for conducting timings is agreed on, scoring and charting plans are set, and time is set aside for teacher-student conferencing.

In special education or remedial settings, the same procedures are established, but it may take more time to select and arrange students' Skill Builder Sheets. IEPs may play a role in which the teacher would have to make sure that the practice activities are matched directly with IEP goals and objectives. Nearly all the materials and procedures recommended for general classroom settings are also appropriate for the special education teacher. If parents are using Skill Builder Sheets, they would need some of the materials required for classrooms; however, the necessary materials are few and easy to obtain.

Materials. Getting started requires some items that are typically found in schools, however the following may have to be sought elsewhere. The following is a starter kit for 30 students:

- 30 individual student manila folders
- 30 sheets of acetate
- 30 plastic-tip pens
- 30 individual sponges
- 30 Academic Charts
- 30 #2 pencils
- One music and tone audiotape (one-minute timed practices)

In addition to the student materials, it would be useful for the teacher to have a stopwatch or a kitchen timer. With the kitchen timer, teachers or students start the timing by touching a button. Some models have a digital display and a programmable beep sound. (A Student Materials Kit, which includes most of the listed materials, is available from Sopris West.)

Packets of Skill Builder Sheets can be chosen from a variety of packets in the curriculum areas of:

- Math
- Language Arts
- Grammar
- Handwriting
- U.S. Map Skills
- Science
- Spelling
- Social Studies

Teachers select individual Skill Builder Sheets from the curriculum packets using the procedures for selecting the skill explained in Chapter 2.

Other Materials. Once the basic materials, including the Skill Builder Sheets, are organized and in place you should consider the following additional supplies:

- File folders to separate sheets by skill area
- File cabinet or plastic file box for storage
- Additional Academic Charts (100 each)
- Additional plastic-tip pens (10 each)

Regular Classroom Daily Routine. One of the keys to successful implementation of *Basic Skill Builders* is establishing a routine for daily practice sessions. Fifteen years of experience has demonstrated to the authors that students must be skilled in taking timed practices, scoring, and then recording their individual performances. Much like practicing a new academic skill, students should also practice the steps in conducting and scoring one-minute timed practices. The following is a typical day:

1. Request that students retrieve their individual folders. Skill folders are constructed by taping a clear piece of acetate to the inside of the folder and an Academic Chart on the outside of the folder. The folders and the charts are labeled with the students' names. The curriculum area (e.g., Math) is written in the lower right corner of the chart. The Skill Sheet is placed under the acetate (see Figure 6-1). The folders can be kept at individual student desks, or at some central location in the classroom.

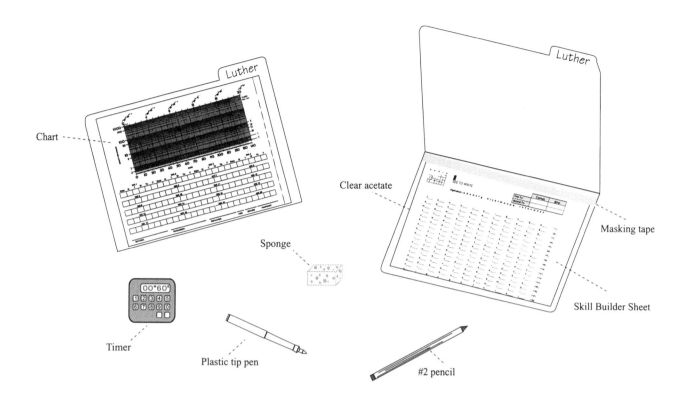

Figure 6-1
Student Folder and Materials

2. Once the folders are available and opened, the students are asked to verify that the appropriate Skill Builder Sheet is properly placed under the clear acetate.

3. Students are reminded that they are to complete as many problems, read as many words, underline as many verbs, write as many letters, etc. as possible during the one-minute timed practice.

4. Two options exist when conducting the one-minute timed practice. First, the teacher instructs the students to "Please begin," and then in 60 seconds says "Thank you." The second choice involves a music or tone audiotape. In this instance, start a tape player and allow the music to run in 60-second intervals, which are marked by a distinct tone or beep. You can also use a tape with no music, just a tone every 60 seconds. Students score and record the number of corrects and errors from their first trial and prepare for a second try. Give students a second try with the same Skill Builder Sheets.

5. Scoring is relatively simple if answer sheets are available. In most situations, Skill Builder Sheets are accompanied by a companion answer sheet that is available on the reverse side. Where there are no available answer sheets, one is prepared and stapled to the back of the Skill Builder Sheets. The answer sheet can be placed under the acetate allowing answers to be quickly scored. If more than one trial is encouraged, students clean the acetate using a

small sponge or paper towel. They record the best of the two trials. (A note on sponges: keep them collected in a jar with an occasional teaspoon of vinegar. This will retain a fresh smell.)

6. The next step is getting the performance data on the chart. If using the Academic Chart, instruct students how to take the raw score (corrects and errors) and write it in the appropriate day-of-the-week box in the lower half of the chart sheet. Next, students are instructed to plot the appropriate day line and frequency line intersection on the chart itself. Often, it is helpful to have students practice on an expanded semi-logarithmic chart before tackling their individual charts. Students can practice finding a series of frequency lines, then practice with days-of-the-week lines. From third grade on, students should be able to do their own charting. Younger grades can chart if something other than a semi-logarithmic chart is used. Be sure to use a #2 pencil when charting because it is difficult, if not impossible, to erase ink.

7. At this point, depending on the overall plan, students can either move on to completing timed practices on other Skill Builder Sheets in other curriculum areas, meet with the teacher for further feedback, or store their folders until they need them again. In any case, teachers should review students' performances at least once a week, and more often if students are at aim or seem to be struggling.

8. One of the most critical elements of the *Basic Skill Builders* model is the immediate feedback and positive reinforcement for students who have demonstrated improvement. Class parties can be held to celebrate those who have reached their aims.

Resource Room Routine. Working with students with special needs requires essentially the same materials and procedures as working with regular classroom students. For example, the difference between managing a group of 30 general classroom students and 15 special education students, is that the latter requires more individual planning. Teaching at-risk and special education students often means more curriculum slice backs, tool skill exercises, opportunities to practice, and more time spent in decision making. Additional procedural differences are:

- In special education classes there are typically fewer students, but they may have highly complex problems. The challenge is to individualize, while at the same time manage the timed practices without constant attention from teachers. It may be helpful to establish an area or station where students can take their timed practices.

- Establishing a Skill Builder Sheets "bank," similar to the one found in regular classrooms, allows for storage of black and white masters, as well as a place for students to maintain their individual folders.

- Once students are familiar with the location of their individual files and the timing procedures, they will become their own best managers.

Home Programs. We mentioned earlier that when parents become involved, they have a better understanding of the classroom program and can provide significant reinforcement to the instructional and curricular objectives. Most important, when parents are involved in helping with classroom objectives, there is much more commitment and carry-over of the newly acquired skills at home.

We know that Skill Builder Sheet practice at home helps students by reinforcing skills taught and practiced in the classroom. Parents, however, must be provided a rationale for fluency and the advantage of one-minute practice sessions. They will also need the materials (folder, pen, chart, etc.) necessary to carry out the plan. A short written guide for conducting timed practices, recording the scores, providing feedback, and communicating with teachers will be very helpful. The brief guide that accompanies the Skill Builders Sheets can serve the purpose of introducing the procedure to parents. Finally, parents should have input when deciding on an incentive plan that links rewards with learning, maintaining, transferring, and generalizing the new skill. When implementing these incentives, be sure to keep students involved when choosing the rewards and reinforcements.

IN SUMMARY

1. Discuss the philosophy, goals, objectives, and activities of *Basic Skill Builders* with administrators, fellow teachers, students, and parents.

2. Select the appropriate task, curriculum area, skill area, Learning Channel, and aim for the entire class.

3. Select the appropriate Skill Builder Sheets and prepare students for repeated one-minute timed practices.

4. Directly and continually monitor students' performance and learning.

5. Decide whether the current instruction or Skill Builder Sheet (curriculum) is appropriate.

6. Manage student plans in regular/special education settings, as well as home programs.

Other Sopris West Publications of Interest

One-Minute Academic Functional Assessment and Interventions: "Can't" Do It . . . or "Won't" Do It?

Joe Witt, Ph.D. and Ray Beck, Ed.D.

Grades K–12

This *One-Minute* assessment process will help you quickly identify the specific causal factors affecting individual student performance. By systematically assessing whether a student "can't" or "won't" do the work, you can determine the appropriate intervention or teaching strategy to implement. You need different intervention strategies for different situations, and this book provides dozens. Includes reproducible forms, worksheets, and checklists.

Math Rescue: Resources for Computation

Larry Bradsby, M.S. and Shirley Bradsby, M.A.

Grades K–6

Help students master computation with more than 600 multisensory activities, coded to skill level, so you can match activities to individual student needs and modality strengths. Six math topics are addressed: modeling addition and subtraction, basic facts of addition and subtraction, addition and subtraction with regrouping, modeling of multiplication and division, basic facts of multiplication and division, and algorithms for multiplication and division.

Assessments and reproducibles included.

REWARDS (Reading Excellence: Word Attack and Rate Development Strategies): The Multisyllabic Word Reading Program

Anita L. Archer, Ph.D.; Mary M. Gleason, Ph.D.; and Vicky Vachon, Ph.D.

Grades 4–12

Help struggling readers meet and surpass grade level expectancies! In this 20-lesson program, a flexible strategy is outlined that can move students from an early elementary reading level to one of increased fluency and comprehension.

Students participating in this program will:

- Decode previously unfamiliar multisyllabic words containing two to eight parts.
- Accurately read more multisyllabic words within one sentence.
- Accurately read more multisyllabic words found in science, social studies, and other classroom materials.
- Read content-area passages accurately and fluently.
- Experience increased comprehension as their accuracy and fluency increase.

Field-tested with positive results in intensive remedial programs as well as in general and special education classes, this program can dramatically improve your students' reading abilities and the quality of their work in other subjects. It can also increase confidence levels.

To order additional copies of the programs described, or for more information call:

800.547.6747